MW00764866

PROPHET OF JUSTICE
PROPHET OF LIFE

PROPHET OF JUSTICE PROPHET OF LIFE

ESSAYS ON
WILLIAM STRINGFELLOW

EDITED BY
ROBERT BOAK SLOCUM

 CHURCH

Church Publishing Incorporated, New York

Library of Congress Cataloging-in-Publication Data

Prophet of justice, prophet of life : essays on William Stringfellow /
    edited by Robert Boak Slocum.

    p.   cm.

    Includes bibliographical references.
    ISBN 0-89869-269-5 (alk. paper)
    1.Stringfellow, William. 2.Christianity and law. I.Slocum,
Robert Boak, 1952- .
BX4827.S84P76 1997   97-34272
230 '. 044' 092--dc21   CIP

Church Publishing Incorporated
445 Fifth Avenue
New York NY 10016

5 4 3 2 1

CONTENTS

ACKNOWLEDGMENTS

First of all, I want to acknowledge the people who got me started on reading Stringfellow. When Don Armentrout and I were putting together *Documents of Witness: A History of the Episcopal Church, 1782-1985* (New York: Church Hymnal Corporation, 1994), Sue Armentrout suggested that we needed to include Stringfellow. I soon found myself with several of his books in my hands. I was at the beginning of an investigation and adventure that is proving much larger than I expected it to be. I also want to acknowledge Mel Vance, a graduate student in the Department of Theology at Marquette University, who suggested that I might want to write on Stringfellow.

This collection has been substantially encouraged by Jim Griffiss and Bill Wylie-Kellermann, both of whom suggested potential contributors. Uncas McThenia has also been most supportive of this project. I want to thank Rodger Patience of Lark's Flight Communications who has provided able technical support in preparing manuscripts for the publisher.

I am dedicating this book to Jim Griffiss, who taught me much about theology in seminary. He challenged me to think theologically, to see the connectedness of theology and the life of prayer, and to apply theology to the questions facing the church and society, all of which helped me better to appreciate Stringfellow.

R.B.S.

PREFACE

Conventional wisdom would say that a preface, like this, is the place to introduce the subject of the study and the different contributors to the collection. I am only going to do that to a limited extent. There is no simple or entirely satisfying answer to the question, "Who was Bill Stringfellow?" Each essay in the collection offers a perspective on the question, and some offer to answer it directly. From my perspective, Stringfellow was a Christian believer who had the courage of his convictions. He was radical. He was a prophet who relentlessly unmasked the guises and principalities of death in church and society. He was a lay person in the Episcopal Church, and the Episcopal Church's most significant theologian in his era. He was an attorney who cared deeply about people and social justice. He was Anthony Towne's close friend. Stringfellow was committed to *life*—life in Christ, life in the world, life's victory over death.

Stringfellow was controversial. Controversy and Stringfellow went hand-in-hand. Even in 1996, I have seen the editor of a popular publication shy away from publishing a short discussion of the controversial *Stringfellow*. Even in this collection, the reader will discover different and at times conflicting viewpoints on Stringfellow. For example, Shattuck and Wylie-Kellermann have different perspectives on Stringfellow relative to the American racial crisis. I am making no attempt to homogenize, categorize, or prioritize the essays in this collection. Together they make a tapestry in which the many threads of Stringfellow's work may be traced. The authors' opinions are their own.

What I *do* want to say in this preface is that the concerns which Stringfellow addressed are still with us. The principalities and powers are still interested most especially in their own preservation, whatever the cost in life. We can see this in society generally, and especially in the church. For example, efforts to use "the system" to force or enforce consensus are still with us. And in parish life the real agenda is often to balance the budget and offend no one. This kind of "inoffensive" gospel has no answer for the radical need that hungers for God's presence. It has no place for any need beyond itself. Its gospel is institutional maintenance. Stringfellow reminds us that this kind of inoffensiveness is very offensive to the gospel. It makes a parody of Christ's love. This kind of institutional "playing it safe" is a most dangerous involvement for us. We need Stringfellow's witness today. We need his prodding to let go of our idols, and we need his reminder that in Christ the powers of death will not overcome us. We need his example to show us how *to risk* faithfully.

It is my hope that the various essays in this collection will continue the renewal of interest in Stringfellow's life and theological witness. We need to hear him.

Robert Boak Slocum
Lake Geneva, Wisconsin
November 1996

WILLIAM STRINGFELLOW
A CHRONOLOGY

April 26, 1928

Born Frank William Stringfellow in Cranston, Rhode Island

1941–1945

Northampton High School, Northampton, Massachusetts
Participates in debate and cheerleading
At age 14 decides not to become a priest

1945–1949

Bates College, Lewiston, Maine
July 22–August 8, 1946, attends the World Conference of
Christian Youth, Oslo, Norway

1950

London School of Economics ("died to career")
Participates in the World Student Christian Federation, traveling
in Europe and Asia

1951–1952

Army supply clerk, Second Armored Division, Germany

1953

Studies one semester at the Episcopal Divinity School, Boston

1953–1956

Harvard Law School
1955, Instructor at Tufts University speech department, Boston
Labor Day, 1956, moves to East Harlem, New York City, at the
invitation of the East Harlem Protestant Parish

1957

Participates in the Chicago Conference on Theology and Law (based on Jacques Ellul's work)

December, resigns from the East Harlem Protestant Parish

1961

April 3, co-founds the law firm of Ellis Stringfellow & Patton

1962

A Private and Public Faith published by William B. Eerdmans Publishing

April 25–26, Panel participant responding to Karl Barth at the University of Chicago

Moves with Anthony Towne to West 79th Street, New York City

1963

Instead of Death published by Seabury Press

January, participates in the National Conference on Religion and Race, Chicago ("The only issue is baptism . . . .")

1964

My People Is the Enemy published by Holt, Rinehart and Winston

Free in Obedience published by Seabury Press

1966

Dissenter in a Great Society published by Holt, Rinehart and Winston

February 2–7, travels to Vietnam en route to New Zealand and Australia

Summer, with Anthony Towne, travels with the circus

1967

January 12–24, second tour of Australia and New Zealand

Count It All Joy published by William B. Eerdmans Publishing

The Bishop Pike Affair (written with Anthony Towne) published by Harper & Row

Autumn, moves to "Eschaton" at Block Island, Rhode Island, with Anthony Towne

1968

January, quits drinking alcohol

Receives Guggenheim Fellowship to write American moral theology

Spring, receives first accurate diagnosis of his illness

October, trial of the "Catonsville Nine" in Maryland; speaks to supporters of the defendants before the trial

November 22, survives radical surgery

1969

Impostors of God: Inquiries into Favorite Idols published by Witness Books

September, Bishop James Pike dies in the Judean wilderness

1970

A Second Birthday published by Doubleday

August 11, Daniel Berrigan arrested by the FBI at "Eschaton," Stringfellow and Towne's home

December 17, indicted with Anthony Towne for harboring a fugitive

1971

Charges dropped while Stringfellow is on a research trip to Israel

Suspect Tenderness (with Anthony Towne) published by Holt, Rinehart and Winston

1972

April 30, delivers sermons in Providence, Rhode Island, advocating the impeachment of President Richard Nixon

1973

Ethic for Christians and Other Aliens in a Strange Land published by Word Books

1976

Canonical lawyer for William Wendt, who is charged with allowing an "irregularly" ordained woman priest to celebrate the eucharist

The Death and Life of Bishop Pike (with Anthony Towne) published by Doubleday

November, elected Second Warden of Block Island

Instead of Death, second edition, published by Seabury Press

1977

Conscience and Obedience published by Word Books

1980

January 28, Anthony Towne dies suddenly and unexpectedly

May, Stringfellow suffers a stroke at home on Block Island

November, runs unsuccessfully for First Warden of Block Island

1982

A Simplicity of Faith: My Experience in Mourning published by Abingdon Press

1984

The Politics of Spirituality published by Westminster Press

1985

March 2, William Stringfellow dies in Providence, Rhode Island

—Compiled by Bill Wylie-Kellermann

"LISTEN TO THIS MAN"
A Parable Before the Powers[1]
BILL WYLIE-KELLERMANN

The theological exploration of biography or the theological reconnaissance of history are apt, and even normative, styles because each is congruent with the definitive New Testament insight and instruction: the Incarnation . . . . *This historic, incarnate activity of the Word of God signifies the militance of the Word of God, both in cosmic dimensions of space and time and in each and every item of created life, including* your *personhood and* your *biography or mine. It is this same basis of the Christian faith that is so often diminished, dismissed, omitted, or ignored when theology is rendered in abstract, hypothesized, propositional or academic models . . . . So, I believe, biography (and history),* any *biography and* every *biography, is inherently theological, in the sense that it contains already—literally by virtue of the Incarnation—the news of the gospel whether or not anyone discerns that. We* are each one of us parables.[2]

In 1962 William Stringfellow sat as a young lawyer, the solitary lay person, on the Chicago panel of theologians which questioned Karl Barth on his famous visit to America. Stringfellow's first question, focused both by Romans 13 and the experience of the German church, concerned the civil captivity of U.S. churches. Having foresworn to criticize the United States, Barth was reluctant to comment, but he indicated his sympathy for the query, saying he liked to hear

Stringfellow speak as he did, adding, "I think we agree." Then, in lieu of an answer, he turned to the audience and urged them, "Listen to this man."[3]

It is interesting that, in the published transcript of that conversation,[4] the University of Chicago Divinity School expunged both of those comments from the official record.

Though he traveled and spoke in university and seminary circles, William Stringfellow was never fully received in the theological academy. He was, perhaps, too hot a potato. Too uncredentialed. Too polemical and provocative. Too political. And yet the diminutive and frail lawyer whom New Testament scholar Walter Wink recently named among "the most significant theologians of the twentieth century," may be on the brink of a theological revival. Virtually out of print since his death more than ten years ago, Stringfellow's work has recently been edited into a one-volume reader.[5] A collection of essays about him has already appeared.[6] In addition to the present volume, at least two more books are in the works. Conferences have been undertaken, and several dissertations relating to him are begun, including one in German. Further, a biography and even a video are in the making.

The moment is right to reconsider Stringfellow's legacy: to listen to him again. Or finally for the first time.

Because so much of what he noticed and named on the horizon has come fully to be, his scathing critique rings true and useful now as when first uttered. Theologically, Stringfellow's most significant contribution was to reappropriate the biblical language of "principalities and powers," opening the door for a new social critique grounded in the New Testament. He thereby effectively altered the landscape of theological ethics, seeding, for example, the superb trilogy on the powers recently completed by Walter Wink.[7] (The thirty-year odyssey of that principalities project was set in motion when Wink set out to review Stringfellow's *Free in Obedience* in 1964.)[8]

As the religious right in America popularizes "spiritual warfare," Stringfellow's work provides a necessary corrective. Though he too took seriously the phenomenon of collective possession and the power of intercession, he was the more scripturally literate. He sought to read America biblically, "*not* the other way around, *not* (to put it in an appropriately awkward way) to construe the Bible Americanly."[9] Where the religious right sees the need for individual piety fused with imperial conformity, he advocated resistance as the only way to live humanly in the midst of death. And so, indeed, he lived.

Who, then, is William Stringfellow? Participant in postwar ecumenism, helping shape the worldwide student Christian movement; 1956 Harvard Law School graduate who took up street law in New York's East Harlem; civil rights activist helping goad white mainstream Christianity into the black freedom struggle of the sixties; early critic of the Vietnam war, visiting there in 1966; notorious interlocutor with Karl Barth in that 1962 American visit; friend, counsel, and biographer of Bishop James Pike; federal indictee charged with harboring Daniel Berrigan while underground in August of 1970; correspondent of Jacques Ellul; subject of FBI surveillance; adviser and canonical defender of the Episcopal women priests irregularly ordained in 1974; caller for the impeachment of Richard Nixon (well before Watergate); reformer and environmental activist in the small-town politics of Block Island; connoisseur of the circus; host and cook extraordinaire; "monastic" contemplative and island recluse; author of sixteen books; parable of the Word of God.

This last phrase is Stringfellow's own, and it is emblematic of his incarnational theology.[10] In his view, every biography is necessarily theological, because it evinces the presence of the Word of God, recognized or not, in the life and personhood of a human being. He took "vocation" to be essentially the name of that personal recognition. His own theological writing was hence substantially autobiographical, with three volumes explicitly comprising a trilogy.[11] The first of these, about the East Harlem experience, he even subtitled, "an autobiographical polemic." That, too, is an evocative phrase. By it I believe he meant to suggest that not only is the Word inherent in our lives, but also that the "principalities and powers" are active characters in the drama. And this is so whether we acknowledge and resist them or succumb to their wiles. Moreover, Stringfellow saw the narrative of his own self-accounting as yet another engagement which carried the struggle a step further, affecting again the exposure of the powers.[12] This is biblically apropos. A gospel, for example, is the good news of Jesus' open confrontation with the rulers and authorities, which is itself—in the retelling of proclamation—a frontal assault on their rule.

In Germany, as a supply clerk with NATO forces in the early fifties, Bill Stringfellow had read the gospels over and over—"in order to keep my sanity." The practice effectively prompted, he once confided, his conversion. Elsewhere he wrote,

> I forebear describing that ordeal for now, except to say that, along the way, I had entered into the reading of the Bible—a bizarre thing for an Episcopalian to do, I know, and a traumatic exploit for anybody. There is, simply, this danger in reading the Bible that one may be emancipated from the jargon, stereotypes, fables, and similar encumbrances of church tradition and hear the Word of God.[13]

Actually, he seemed to place his conversion at different moments and occasions. Once he located it at a Student Christian Movement conference, involving an intense romantic relationship accompanied, again, with the reading of scripture. Or he wrote that it transpired when he was studying for a year (1950) at the London School of Economics, whereupon he died to career and political ambition.[14] This is not to suggest that his conversion was vague or some sort of a moving target, but that—because he understood it as the restoration and renewal of one's identity in the Word of God—it was for him continually at issue, implicated in the crises and decisions of life.

The London School reference is noteworthy because here he intimates the conjunction of conversion with a freedom from the powers. Career (as distinct from vocation) was itself in Stringfellow's view a principality. Whether self-constructed or institutionalized in a profession, it was subject to idolatry. People give themselves over to careers in self-sacrifice. There they seek justification, meaning, and personal identity. William Stringfellow's conversion involved dying out from under such claims into a gospel freedom.

This freedom was verified promptly. It served him next at Harvard where he effectively slipped the grip of the legal powers. The "spiritual formation," actually a de-formation, inherent in a Harvard Law degree is both brutal and seductive.[15] Stringfellow seemed, indeed, to pass through unscathed. His commitment to the degree was surprisingly minimal: while there, he lived for a time at Episcopal

Divinity School, attending theology courses, taught speech at Tufts University, was on the road with the Student Christian Movement, and organized the first in a series of conferences on law and theology—one of which was instrumental in introducing Jacques Ellul to American lawyers. He was hardly a model law student. Little wonder he was free to ignore completely the sort of Wall Street law career for which he was poised and, instead, make directly for East Harlem.

Recently, his former law partner mentioned Bill to another New York attorney who shook his head with dismay and sighed, "What a wasted life."[16] Well, from the perspective of the legal principalities, perhaps just so. The East Harlem decision was really the first big choice for the margin, for the underside as social location. It was the first self-conscious bad career move. The East Harlem years (1956-1963) were important for a variety of reasons, not the least of which was that there Stringfellow developed theologically his comprehension of the principalities. In a sense, the encounter was unavoidable. He met them literally on the street in authorities, agencies, and bureaucracies:

> Slowly I learned something which folk indigenous to the ghetto know: namely, that the power and purpose of death are incarnated in institutions and structures, procedures and regimes—Consolidated Edison or the Department of Welfare, the Mafia or the police, the Housing Authority or the social work bureaucracy, the hospital system or the banks, liberal philanthropy or corporate real estate speculation. In the wisdom of the people of the East Harlem neighborhood, such principalities are identified as demonic powers because of the relentless and ruthless dehumanization which they cause.[17]

When Karl Barth (one of the few academic theologians to acknowledge William Stringfellow) showed up in America, he came to "the notorious district of East Harlem, north of Manhattan" and was guided through it, as he aptly put it, "under the safe conduct"[18] of Stringfellow. Bill, for his part, knew precisely what he wanted to discuss when time came for their public conversation in Chicago: nothing less than the principalities and powers. His questions, prefaced and nuanced, were nearly as edifying as Barth's answers. They set the agenda for his own writing and thinking in the years to come:

> What there is of Protestant moral theology in America almost
> utterly ignores the attempt to account for, explicate, and relate
> one's self to the principalities and powers. Yet, empirically more
> and more, the principalities and powers seem to have an aggres-
> sive, indeed, possessive, ascendancy in American life—including,
> alas, the life of the American churches. Who are these principali-
> ties and powers? What is their significance in the creation and in
> the fall? What significance do they have with respect to merely
> human sin? What is their relation to the claim that Christ is the
> Lord of history? What is the relation of the power and presence
> of death in history to the principalities and powers, and therefore,
> practically speaking, what freedom does a Christian have from
> the dominion of all of these principalities and powers?"[19]

Virtually all of these questions would be raised in his mind concerning one of the most formidable principalities Stringfellow
encountered in Harlem: racism. He acknowledged it essentially as an
idolatry possessing a whole class or race of human beings who pre-
tended justification at the expense of another.[20] This idol so supplants
and preempts the justification of Jesus Christ that it may be recognized as a theological affront to baptism which is "the sacrament of
the unity of all people in Christ."[21] Candidly, he beheld its ascendan-
cy in a church which had surrendered to the assaults and seductions
of its rule.

In January of 1963, Bill Stringfellow created a small uproar speaking at the National Conference on Religion and Race. Chaired by
Benjamin Mays and headlined by Martin King, Sergeant Shriver, and
Abraham Heschel, among others, it was the first major ecumenical
foray into the racial crisis. A response to the address of Dr. Heschel,
Stringfellow's remarks were controversial in part because he excoriated the gathering as "too little, too late, and too lily white" (a phrase he
would come regularly to employ in prodding the church), because he
observed that the initiative in the struggle did not reside with white
folk, but had passed from white to black, and because he named voices (like Malcolm X and James Baldwin) who would not be heard there.
However, his most remarkable and prophetic observations were these:

> The monstrous American heresy is in thinking that the whole drama
> of history takes place between God and men. But the truth,
> Biblically and theologically and empirically is quite otherwise: the

drama of this history takes place amongst God and men and the principalities and powers, the great institutions and ideologies active in the world. It is the corruption and shallowness of humanism which beguiles Jew or Christian into believing that men are masters of institution or ideology. Or to put it differently, racism is not an evil in the hearts or minds of men, racism is a principality, a demonic power, a representative image, an embodiment of death, over which men have little or no control, but which works its awful influence in the lives of men.[22]

Since this is a power already confronted and overcome by Jesus Christ, Stringfellow concluded, the real issue (perchance the only issue) is baptism—its meaning as the sacrament of unity and the freedom of reconciliation.[23]

Another, but not unrelated, matter from the Harlem years involved his resignation from the East Harlem Protestant Parish. Stringfellow had come at the invitation of the Parish, had enjoyed their sanction and support, and worked from their base. And yet, though he remained thereafter to work in Harlem, within a year and a half he had quit the group ministry. His letter of resignation (duplicated on the Parish's own ditto machine, widely circulated, and subsequently in essence published in *My People Is the Enemy*[24]) articulated several theological reasons for his separation. Specifically, they involved the neglect of the Bible in common life and a disempowerment of the laity. Stringfellow's letter of resignation anticipated in a striking way his reflection on the church in relation to the powers. He regarded the church as possessing a vocation to be the "exemplary principality," the one not bound to the ethic of survival, the institution specifically free to die—to risk itself completely for the life of the world.[25] It seems he saw the Parish in its aspect as a principality, noting how some in the group entertained the "pompous superstition" that the group ministry itself represented "the New Jerusalem."[26] And yet the energy put into its maintenance and survival instead inhibited life and ministry in the storefront congregations: "The paradox of the group ministry, as it actually operates here, is that it is the chief and constant threat to the emergence of living congregations among the people of the neighborhood while at the same time the emergence of some congregations here is the most substantial threat to the group ministry."[27] He urged that the surest sign of freedom among the clerical leadership "will be when all of its members are willing even to give up the group ministry."[28]

Let it be said that the East Harlem Protestant Parish was the vanguard of an urban ministry revival movement in America, a model of evangelism and ecclesiology. In later years, Stringfellow would regularly include "movements" among his exhaustive lists of the powers, along with all images, institutions, traditions and the like. For those of us who work for and yearn toward movements of social transformation, he puts his finger on an edifying paradox: the fallen bondage of the best we do and the freedom to die.

Bill Stringfellow was himself free to die. And he came near to death with some frequency.[29] The most notorious occasion was connected with radical surgery in 1968. Years prior on a World Student Christian Federation trip to India, he had contracted hepatitis and, while in law school, suffered a series of gall-bladder attacks. He even missed graduation to go under the surgeon's knife. In the late sixties, however, his health began mysteriously to fail. He'd been abusing alcohol for some time, but that did not explain the weight loss and excruciating back pain. In fact, his pancreas had ceased to work, and William Stringfellow was slowly starving to death. The remedy was an experimental and high-risk surgery removing the organ altogether. The consequences of that surgery were that he was, ever after, completely dependent on taking animal enzymes each time he ate in order to digest his food. Since they are less efficient, he was required each day to consume meals totaling 8,000 to 9,000 calories in order to assimilate 1,500. Moreover, it rendered him a total diabetic, which dictated a regimen of insulin injections and balancing the dietary intake with precarious sugar needs. Over the long haul, the diabetes also worked its degenerative effects: loss of circulation—especially in his legs, diminished eyesight, episodes of insulin shock and diabetic coma, plus a stroke—all of which he weathered in prayer and cursing.

Such a configuration of ailments and pain did not much constrain the pace of his travel and speaking or inhibit his writing. "My head is still working," he would say. Illness did, however, limit the sort of public resistance in which he could engage. It would have been unwise, deadly even, to risk jail in the direct action way many of his civil rights and antiwar friends were able. He lamented this. Yet in a certain sense Stringfellow's infirmity was his imprisonment. As he put it, in severe pain, to Bishop James Pike then anointing him in the ancient rite of divine unction immediately after the 1968 surgery, "My illness is a preparation for the concentration camp."[30]

William Stringfellow lived with death as a kind of enemy in constant accompaniment. He knew death as an intimate and named it in personal and public guises. He walked with it in death's pervasive geography: on the street, among the principalities, up close in illness. He recognized in each the same power.

> The decade [of the sixties] locates me, at its outset, deeply in the midst of work as a white lawyer in Harlem, but it closes in fragile survival of prolonged, obstinate, desperate illness. It begins in social crisis, it ends in personal crisis. For me, these are equally profound *because* the aggression of death is the moral reality pervasive in both and, moreover, the grace to confront and transcend death is the same in each crisis.[31]

Bill claimed to have learned the freedom of grace from the people of Harlem. But he also knew it at least since the freedom he experienced at the London School. And it came into sharp focus in the decision to undergo radical surgery. It was, personally, the freedom to die. Thus, the decision amid pain and the temptation to despair was, he reports, quite lucid and even matter-of-fact. "I felt like a human being. I felt free."[32]

Inevitably, he comprehended the political significance of that freedom. Just a month earlier, Stringfellow had attended the trial of the Catonsville Nine. Dan and Phil Berrigan, among others, had burned draft files with homemade napalm in a liturgical act of protest against the war in Vietnam. Bill would later refer to this as a "politically informed exorcism."[33] Concurrent with the trial there was a festival of hope: music, poetry, and words of encouragement to continued resistance were offered in the sanctuary of a Baltimore church. Stringfellow, who could barely walk from pain, was summoned to the pulpit for a word. He offered an admonition, a benediction, an utterance of the gospel:

> Remember, now, that the State has only one power it can use against human beings: death. The State can persecute you, prosecute you, imprison you, exile you, execute you. All of these mean

the same thing. The State can consign you to death. The grace of Jesus Christ in this life is that death fails. There is nothing the State can do to you, or to me, which we need fear.[34]

The Nine, as it proved, were convicted, but several of them declined to submit readily to sentence. Daniel Berrigan went underground, speaking, writing, and playfully eluding the Federal authorities for several months. He was a walking festival of hope. Dan was finally captured by the FBI at the Block Island home of William Stringfellow and Anthony Towne. In consequence the two were indicted and charged with harboring a fugitive.

Though the indictment, clearly a political charge, was eventually quashed, I believe this was a momentous event in Stringfellow's life. It was the first time he had personally suffered so bluntly the aggressions of the principalities. Given his state of health, it was indeed a bodily assault threatening death. But it was also his first experience of being victimized by the legal principalities. In many respects the event seeded the energy of what may be his finest book, *An Ethic for Christians and Other Aliens in a Strange Land*. As it happened, Bill and Dan had sat at the dining room table discussing the biblical bases of that book (the Babylon texts of Revelation) while in all likelihood the FBI listened in by high-powered directional microphone. Then came the indictment, a provocation further illuminating the texts, clarifying the mind. If the principalities and powers had known what they were doing, they would have let it slide. That book effected their complete exposure (and became a theological handbook of the American resistance movement). Stringfellow claimed yet again the grace and freedom he commended. He was unintimidated, standing instead by his friendship with Berrigan. He even seemed at some level to enjoy being indicted for an explicitly Christian virtue: the practice of hospitality.

Stringfellow and Towne shared a charism for hospitality. They had moved to Block Island—some thirteen miles off the coast—in the wake of Bill's surgery. As for Berrigan—and many others, myself included—this monastic retreat, which they dubbed "Eschaton," was a respite, a place of spiritual and theological refreshment. The table was spread—the Bible, the Book of Common Prayer, and the *New York Times* were open.

Fittingly, Bill and Anthony's association began in an occasion of hospitality in the early sixties. If truth be told, Towne had retained Stringfellow to prevent his eviction, but Bill neglected the proceedings. On the day of the eviction, Anthony showed up on the attorney's doorstep in distress. They returned to salvage his essential belongings, and thereafter Bill offered his own place as temporary shelter. Before long, as such things go, "our acquaintance became friendship, then eventually, community."[35]

Their ministry of hospitality was first taken up in a Manhattan apartment—something of a theological "salon." Activists, church-types, poets, mendicants, pastoral counselees, in endless lot passed through or "crashed." The place served for organizational meetings, fundraisers, and not a few parties. Meanwhile, the speaking and writing. No doubt the pace contributed to Bill's gathering health crisis. The move to Block Island slowed things to a degree, but the vocation of hospitality continued albeit in a more monastic vein.

A word further about William Stringfellow, the theologian, and Anthony Towne, the poet. They were partners in every respect. When Bill writes of their friendship becoming community, or calls Anthony his "sweet companion for seventeen years,"[36] he is being slightly oblique. They had fallen in love. For a certain circle of acquaintances, their moving in together in 1962 was "coming out," the public acknowledgment of Stringfellow's homosexuality. But a much wider circle would have been, and still may be, astonished to hear it. He was, as one friend put it, "almost but not quite not out."[37] That is not to minimize the weight of this decision which represented, nevertheless, a further commitment to the social margin, yet another bad career move.

For years as an attorney, Stringfellow had represented homosexuals in court cases as counsel for both the Mattachine Society and for the George Henry Foundation.[38] However, when he wrote or spoke about the topic (as, for example, with *Instead of Death*,[39] which he was writing at the time of his romance with Anthony in 1962, or when he addressed the National Convention of Integrity[40] in 1979) he did not identify himself as a gay man. Even after the Stonewall riot of 1968 which initiated the Gay Rights movement, and after prominent Episcopalians, for example among the first women priests, had come out at the 1979 General Convention in Denver, he remained circumspect and quite private. Still, he was able to articulate with candid accuracy the suffering of homosexuals:

> Many, perhaps essentially among churchpeople, will still find homosexual relations personally incomprehensible, aesthetically abhorrent, and morally reprehensible. Be that as it may, more fundamental issues than those of personal distaste are involved in the practice of homosexuality. Homosexuals are often tempted to suicide, experience desperate identity crises, sometimes are victims of extortion or blackmail, live in fear of exposure and social disgrace, suffer much from profound and unabsolved guilt, are readily vulnerable to venereal disease, feel more persecuted than other social minorities, perhaps have endured the collapse of relationships with parents and families, may—despite lots of sex— have never known love. These are the significant personal and social issues of homosexuality.[41]

As to the principalities involved, homophobia must be named, though Stringfellow spoke of it rather as the church's league with the "worldly institutions of marriage and family, profoundly distorting the gospel's view of these powers."[42] And if he never confronted and rebuked those powers in a way that openly risked his own vulnerability, still he came to a peacefulness about his own identity, a freedom he identified once again with conversion.

> The new life in Christ means, for our minds and our bodies and for any of our abilities, that we have the exceptional freedom to be who we are and thus to welcome and affirm our sexuality as a gift, absolved from guilt or embarrassment or shame; to be liberated in our sexuality from self-indulgence or lust; to be free to love with wholeness as persons and to recognize and identify and embrace the same wholeness in others . . .[43]

Stringfellow would not have regarded his relationship with Anthony as essentially sexual. They were partners in so many respects: in literary, theological, culinary, economic, intercessory, and political collaboration. An elegant writer himself (they co-authored several books), Towne was a good editor of Stringfellow. They shared as well a common love for the circus, and one summer packed up a station wagon to travel for several weeks with the Clyde Beatty–Cole

Bros. entourage through New England. Anthony's sudden death in 1980 signified another vocational crisis for Stringfellow, implicating once again his conversion. The account of that is told in what is certainly, by structure and content, his most beautiful book. It's full of love. It is a pastoral tome on grief and mourning. And it claims once again in concrete relationship a freedom from the bondage of death, the freedom of the resurrection.

Simplicity of Faith also narrates another love, the story of Stringfellow's involvement in the life of Block Island, a community of some 400 year-round residents (plus many thousands of summer visitors.) His participation was remarkably similar to his life and work in the East Harlem ghetto. He was active in Island politics, even serving for a term as Second Warden (vice-mayor) on the Town Council. His love for people on the Island and for that bit of land itself comes through. He spent himself actively defending it against the ravages of overdevelopment.

One book Stringfellow left unfinished at the time of his death concerned baptism. He had given some lectures to an American Baptist conference and agreed to expand them for publication by Judson Press. He smiled to think of an Episcopalian explaining baptism to the Baptists, but didn't hesitate before the task. Indeed, he confessed that theologically he might fairly be thought "a closet Anabaptist."[44]

He explained that baptism marked new citizens in Christ, preempting the old citizenship of Caesar by confessing the sovereignty of the Word of God in history over the pretensions of any power or regime. He saw the apostolic precedent of that in Pentecost.

> The scene, as we learn of it from the book of the Acts of the Apostles, is not private, but quite public; it is not individualistic but notorious, not idiosyncratic, but scandalous; and onlookers are said to behold Pentecost as provocative and controversial; it appears to have been an offense to the ruling authorities. Central in the experience of the power of the Holy Spirit among the disciples, both commonly and severally, is a transcendence of worldly distinction (as race, age, sex, class, occupation, nationality, language, tongue) that anticipates the eschatological consummation of the whole of fallen creation in the Kingdom of God.[45]

The witness of William Stringfellow's life indeed anticipated that consummation. He died March 2, 1985, at the age of fifty-six. His ashes were buried next to Anthony's on the bluff overlooking the Atlantic. Close on a wall is a plaque which reads, "Near this cottage the remains of William Stringfellow and Anthony Towne await the resurrection." Alleluia.

NOTES

1 A seminal version of this essay appeared in the Australian ethics magazine, *Faith and Freedom* (March 1995). This essay is expanded and adapted from one which appeared in *Theology Today* (October 1996).

2 William Stringfellow, *A Simplicity of Faith: My Experience in Mourning* (Nashville: Abingdon Press, 1982), 20.

3 From master tape recording of the event held by Word Record and Music Group, Nashville. In the forward to *Evangelical Theology: An Introduction* (Grand Rapids, Michigan: William B. Eerdmans Publishing, 1963), the lectures which Barth gave at the University of Chicago and Princeton University, he refers to "the conscientious and thoughtful New York attorney William Stringfellow who caught my attention more than any other person" (ix).

4 "Introduction to Theology," *Criterion* 2:1 (Winter 1963), 22.

5 Bill Wylie-Kellermann, ed., *A Keeper of the Word* (Grand Rapids, Michigan: William B. Eerdmans Publishing, 1994).

6 Andrew McThenia, ed., *Radical Christian and Exemplary Lawyer* (Grand Rapids, Michigan: William B. Eerdmans Publishing, 1995).

7 Walter Wink, *Naming the Powers* (Philadelphia: Fortress Press, 1984); idem, *Unmasking the Powers* (Philadelphia: Fortress Press, 1986); idem, *Engaging the Powers* (Minneapolis: Fortress Press, 1992).

8 Walter Wink, "Stringfellow on the Powers," in McThenia, *Radical Christian and Exemplary Lawyer*, 25.

9 William Stringfellow, *An Ethic for Christians and Other Aliens in a Strange Land* (Waco Texas: Word Books, 1973), 13.

10 Stringfellow, *A Simplicity of Faith*, 20.

11 William Stringfellow, *My People Is the Enemy* (New York: Holt, Rinehart and Winston, 1964); idem, *A Second Birthday*, (New York: Doubleday, 1970); idem, *A Simplicity of Faith* (1982).

12 In a certain sense, Stringfellow had begun applying to his own life something of the same hermeneutic he was developing with regard to the scriptures. Plainly put, he viewed the powers as intervening and imposing themselves on the latter. He saw the Bible widely read in captivity to the principalities, read in the service of empire, read (as he put it) Americanly. The ethical task, like the hermeneutical one, involved breaking and transcending their spiritual grasp. See Bill Wylie-Kellermann, "Bill, the Bible, and the Seminary Underground," in Andrew W. McThenia, Jr., ed., *Radical Christian and Exemplary Lawyer*, 56-72; also Bill Wylie-Kellermann, "Listening Against Babel," *A Keeper of the Word*, 182-83; idem, introduction to a previously unpublished Bible study guide, "Advent 1982: Preparing for the Coming of the Lord."

13 Stringfellow, *A Second Birthday*, 144.

14 Stringfellow, *A Simplicity of Faith*, 125.

15 Ibid., 126-27: "Initiation into the legal profession, as it is played out at a place like the Harvard Law School, is, as one would expect, elaborately mythologizied, asserts an aura of tradition, and retains a reputation for civility. All of these insinuate that this process is benign, though, both empirically and in principal, it is demonic."

16 Interview of William Ellis by Andrew W. McThenia, Jr., New York City, June 3, 1993.

17 Stringfellow, *Instead of Death* (New York: Seabury Press, 1976), 5.

18 Eberhard Busch, *Karl Barth: His Life from Letters and Autobiographical Texts* (Grand Rapids, Michigan: William B. Eerdmans Publishing, 1994), 460.

19 "Introduction to Theology," 23. Pertinent portions of the *Criterion* (Winter 1963) transcript are also reproduced in Wylie-Kellermann, *A Keeper of the Word*, 187-91.

20 William Stringfellow, *Imposters of God: Inquiries into Favorite Idols* (Dayton, Ohio: Geo. A. Pflaum, 1969), 80.

21 William Stringfellow, *Free in Obedience* (New York: Seabury Press, 1964), 77. In this sense he anticipated the treatment of racism as the confessional issue it came to be in South Africa. See John DeGruchy and Charles Villa-Vincencio, eds., *Apartheid is a Heresy* (Capetown: David Philip, 1983).

22 Transcript of his talk, published as "Care Enough to Weep," *The Witness* (February 21, 1963), 14.

23 Will Campbell recounts the uproar Stringfellow's remarks caused among Jewish participants in *Brother to a Dragonfly* (New York: Seabury Press, 1977), 229-30. More positive reaction to his controversial address may be found in Benjamin E. Mays, *Born to Rebel: an Autobiography* (New York: Scribner's, 1971), 263 and Anna Arnold Hedgeman, *The Trumpet Sounds: A Memoir of Negro Leadership* (New York: Holt, Rinehart and Winston), 3.

24 Stringfellow, *My People Is the Enemy*, 85-97. Stringfellow's original resignation letter (April 2, 1958) is in box 35 of the William Stringfellow Papers (collection #4438 in the Rare and Manuscript Collections Div. of Olin Library, Cornell University, Ithaca, New York).

25 Stringfellow, *A Second Birthday*, 143-148.

26 Stringfellow, resignation letter, 6; cf. idem, *An Ethic for Christians and Other Aliens in a Strange Land* (Waco, Texas: Word, 1973), 51.

27 Stringfellow, resignation letter, 3.

28 Ibid., 6.

29 A later occasion is described in Stringfellow, *A Simplicity of Faith*, 62 ff.

30 Stringfellow, "Harlem, Rebellion, and Resurrection," *Christian Century* (Dec. 11, 1970), 1348: "The bishop understood, I am sure, that I meant this to be a cheerful comment."

31 Ibid., 1346.

32 Stringfellow, *A Second Birthday*, 98.

33 Stringfellow, *An Ethic for Christians*, 150.

34 Stringfellow, *A Second Birthday*, 33.

35 Stringfellow, *A Simplicity of Faith*, 48.

36 Ibid., 115.

37 Andrew W. Mcthenia, Jr., "How This Celebration Began," *Radical Christian and Exemplary Lawyer,* 15.

38 Stringfellow, *My People Is the Enemy*, 42, 58-60.

39 William Stringfellow, *Instead of Death* (New York: Seabury Press, 1963), 34-35. His comments remained unchanged in the expanded edition of 1976.

40 William Stringfellow, "An Exhortation to Integrity," *Keeper of the Word*, 331-34.

41 Stringfellow, *Instead of Death* (1963), 35. The passage is essentially unchanged in the 1976 edition.

42 Stringfellow, "An Exhortation to Integrity," 333.

43 Ibid., 332.

44 William Stringfellow, "Authority in Baptism: The Vocation of Jesus and the Ministry of the Laity," in Wylie-Kellermann, ed., *Keeper of the Word*, 158.

45 Ibid., 160.

WILLIAM STRINGFELLOW
AND THE CHRISTIAN WITNESS
AGAINST DEATH[1]

ROBERT BOAK SLOCUM

William Stringfellow (1928-1985), an Episcopal layman, was perhaps the most important American theologian of this century. He encountered the social issues of his day with a faith that was clear, articulate, passionate, and biblical. He identified the power of death in the many forms (personal and social) that threaten to diminish humanity through fear, intimidation, bigotry, greed, hate, domination, or anything less than God that would become a "ruling idol" in human hearts. Stringfellow resisted those threats in light of the victory of life over death in Christ. He was unwavering in the face of opposition and controversy, even when his support and assistance to Daniel Berrigan brought the threat of federal prosecution. Stringfellow would not be intimidated, silenced, or deterred from the Christian ethic of witness against death in all its forms. He encountered the forms and powers of death with a theological critique and personal witness that reached far beyond the issues of his time.

Unfortunately, Stringfellow's theology has been something of a critical enigma, and the significance of his work has not been fully recognized. Walter Wink, a seminary professor of biblical interpretation and a supporter of Stringfellow, notes that "He has been largely ignored by academic theologians and, when recognized at all, introduced by the sobriquet, 'William Stringfellow, the noted lay theologian,' meaning by that not simply non-ordained, but amateur, untrained, uncredentialed, and illegitimate."[2] Wink adds that many dismissed Stringfellow as a "popularizer." Wink also observes that, "Because he wrote for an audience of his peers—and he regarded everyone as his peer—Stringfellow's books were not laden with footnotes, jargon, dense and convoluted arguments, or discussions about other authors."[3] Stringfellow certainly wrote theology for the widest possible audience. For example, *Instead of Death* was originally written as a "short studybook" for use in the Episcopal Church's curriculum for high school youth.[4] The book is simple, powerful, practical, and uncompromising in its articulation of Stringfellow's theology of life and death. The significance of Stringfellow's theology was enhanced, not diminished, by its clarity and applicability to daily life.

Others viewed Stringfellow's theology with enthusiasm. Jim Wallis, editor of *Sojourners,* states that William Stringfellow "was, in my opinion, the most significant American theologian of the last few decades."[5] Wink considers Stringfellow "America's most important theologian."[6] And Wallis also notes that, "When Karl Barth visited the United States in the early sixties, he called William Stringfellow 'the man America should be listening to.'"[7] In the sixties, as at other times, America needed to take the threat of death seriously. H. Coleman McGehee, Jr., Episcopal Bishop of Michigan, describes Stringfellow as "one of the most authentic prophets of our place and time," and notes that "Both Karl Barth and Jacques Ellul recognized in Stringfellow a peer in prophecy, one who applied the merciless plumbline of scripture to the jerry-built structures of society."[8] Stringfellow was an unflinching prophet against the ravages of death in his world.

A VOICE TO CONTRADICT DEATH

The context and meaning of Stringfellow's Christian witness against death can be brought into focus by the events that were happening in his life in November 1968. At this time the United States was convulsed by protests against American military involvement in Vietnam and controversy over the civil rights movement. Daniel Berrigan, a Jesuit priest and a personal friend of Stringfellow, was arrested with others for burning draft records with napalm in Catonsville, Maryland, and put on trial in Baltimore in November 1968. In November 1968, Stringfellow was living with his close friend Anthony Towne on Block Island (New Shoreham), an island off the coast of Rhode Island. Stringfellow and Towne understood their home as an intentional Christian community, and they eventually named it "Eschaton." It was a place of Christian friendship and hospitality, and they often entertained guests and "pilgrims"—including, from time to time, Daniel Berrigan.

One of the reasons for Stringfellow's move to Block Island was his failing health. He suffered greatly from a disease of the pancreas that brought him to the verge of death in 1968. Stringfellow tried to resist the effects of the disease and maintain his active schedule. However, he underwent an extensive and radical surgery in November 1968. Although Stringfellow came away from that operation with a "wildly erratic diabetes," he surprised many by surviving the surgery and the effects of the illness for many years.[9] Stringfellow describes his medical ordeal in *A Second Birthday*.[10] Anthony Towne, Stringfellow's companion, recalls that shortly before the surgery Stringfellow went to Baltimore for the Berrigan trial: "On the evening of the third day of the trial, what remained of William Stringfellow did, in fact, appear. There were speeches being made to several thousands gathered in a Baltimore church. Stringfellow would utter (whisper) a few words, the last of them an admonition to remember that death has no dominion over us."[11]

After the surgery, Stringfellow returned to live and recuperate on Block Island. Berrigan was convicted of the federal charges against him, and his legal appeal was unsuccessful. However, Berrigan refused to surrender himself to federal authorities after his appeal was denied. He went into hiding "underground." In August 1970 he fled to Eschaton, where Stringfellow and Towne offered him hospitality. Berrigan was arrested at their home several days later.

Before Berrigan's arrest, federal agents posed as "bird watchers" to keep Eschaton under surveillance. Stringfellow and Towne were indicted for "harboring and concealing" the fugitive Berrigan, but these charges were later dismissed on procedural grounds. Stringfellow was warned by friends to keep silent while he was subject to being recharged, but he refused. Berrigan later published a book of poems titled *Block Island,* dedicated to Stringfellow.[12] A line from one of Berrigan's poems provided the title for Stringfellow and Towne's *Suspect Tenderness,* which is a collection of writings that concern the Berrigan witness and the incident at Block Island. Stringfellow also reports that an encounter with a federal agent at this time "contributed" to his conviction to write *Conscience and Obedience.*[13]

Stringfellow perceived the power of death at work in his body and in his society. And he fought that power. One friend notes that "Stringfellow fiercely resented the ravages of disease upon his body. He fought them zealously and insisted on maintaining a travel, lecture, and writing schedule that defied their power—successfully for most of the time."[14] Stringfellow explains that "I resist the power of death and that which, in the somewhat pathetic state of my health, manifestly foreshadows death-like amputation of a leg or two."[15] Concerning the federal charges against him for the Block Island episode, Stringfellow felt he was "being threatened with death" by the American legal system.[16] When Stringfellow spoke to the crowd on the third day of Berrigan's trial in Baltimore, Berrigan noted that "William Stringfellow's life had been on the line for a very long time."[17] Stringfellow understood "death" and the threat of death with a broad meaning, which will be discussed in this article. Stringfellow believed that the powers of death (in whatever form) must have no dominion over us.

Stringfellow's theology was in the spirit of Thomas Merton's presentation of the struggle with the powers of death within the individual and in society. Like Merton, Stringfellow perceived a deep and powerful connection between Christian spirituality and the Christian vocation to resist death. Stringfellow and Merton shared a witness against the powers and disguises of death in the world. Stringfellow dedicated *An Ethic for Christians and Other Aliens in a Strange Land* to Merton. He could easily have joined with Merton in saying that "Life and death are at war within us."[18] In *The Politics of Spirituality,* Stringfellow even discusses the "monastic tactics" of intercession and eucharistic praise of the Word of God as "especially suited to political resistance."[19] Similarly, in *A Simplicity of Faith,* Stringfellow states that "the practice of prayer is *essentially* political—a matter of attention to events and of intercession and advocacy for the needs of human life and of the life of the whole Creation."[20] Prayer is thus an "audacious" political action, "bridging the gap between immediate realities and ultimate hope, between ethics and eschatology, between the world as it is and the Kingdom which is vouchsafed."[21] Stringfellow encountered death with prayer, drawing on all life to overcome death. For Stringfellow, prayer was not "personal" in an isolated and individual sense, but "so personal that it reveals . . . every connection with everyone and everything else in the whole of Creation throughout time."[22] He encountered death with prayer.

THE POWER AND PERVASIVENESS OF DEATH

In addition to death's physiological threat to existence and vitality, Stringfellow perceived the threat of death in the allure of anything less than God to command the worship and praise due only to God. Stringfellow notes that "Death is the obvious meaning of existence, if God is ignored, surviving as death does every other personal or social reality to which is attributed the meaning of existence in this world."[23] He also discusses the power and pervasiveness of death in terms of the Fall, stating that "In the Fall, death reigns over men and nations and ideas, and over all that is, as a living, militant, pervasive and, apparently, ultimate power—in other words, as *that* which gives moral significance to everyone and everything else."[24] Death then becomes the ultimate idol as it takes the place of God, commanding its own worship and conferring its own ultimate meaning. Stringfellow found the idolatry of death to be "pervasive" in American society.[25] He explains that "Death is the ruling idol which all other idols—race, nationalism, religion, money, sex, and all their counterparts—worship and serve, and to which men in their turn give honor and sacrifice through their idolatries."[26]

This idolatrous process of making a substitute for God is visible when people seek to act as God. Stringfellow urges that "Sin is the denunciation of the freedom of God to judge humans as it pleases him to judge them. Sin is the displacement of God's will with one's own will. Sin is the radical confusion as to whether God or the human being is morally sovereign in history."[27] When people or causes arrogate this capacity for ultimate judgment, Stringfellow explains, the outcome is "acute estrangement" and alienation from God and from life itself, leaving them "consigned to death, committed to the service of death, unable to save themselves from death."[28]

Ironically, human overreaching causes a loss of identity instead of an expansion of personal authority and freedom. Stringfellow urges that "the dread of death paradoxically becomes a dread of living."[29] Death thus threatens us with the absence of life, even while our mortal existence continues. Death is the "power abrasively addressing every person in one's own existence with the word that one is not only eventually and finally, but even now and already, estranged, separated, alienated, lost in relationships with everybody and everything else, and—what is very much worse—one's very own self."[30] Death, Stringfellow concludes, "means a total loss of identity."[31] And the solution that death offers for this predicament is idolatry in its many forms. He warns that "the last temptation (in truth, the *only* one) is to suppose that we can help ourselves by worshiping death, after the manner of the principalities and powers."[32]

The power of death is also evident in the institutions and abuses that seek to overturn God and dehumanize the people of God's creation. Stringfellow points to the "social forms of death" in American subcultures, "noticeably those of elderly citizens, of ghettoized blacks, of prison inmates, and of servicemen and Vietnam veterans," in which "the banishment or abandonment of human beings to loneliness, isolation, ostracism, impoverishment, unemployability, separation" become "so dehumanizing that the victims suffer few illusions about their consignment to death or to these moral equivalents of death by American society."[33] Such injustice is not merely a social wrong that should be reformed—although it *is* wrong, and it *should* be reformed! Stringfellow's theology goes beyond social reform and political dissent. He defines abuses against God's sovereignty and the welfare of humanity as *blasphemy*. Stringfellow notes that "the biblical witness not only stands against tyranny and oppression as such but comprehends tyranny and oppression as blasphemy, that is, as the repudiation and defamation of the Lordship of Christ in common history by the ruling powers and political principalities."[34]

Institutions that dehumanize and abuse become "principalities" of death, and seek to make a hideous substitution for the right moral order and dominion of God. For example, recalling his indictment with Towne "for harboring Daniel Berrigan, the fugitive priest," Stringfellow states, "That was how we learned, firsthand, of the chill of death incarnated politically in the perversion of the legal process."[35] And people may become enthralled by those principalities. Stringfellow urges that "Death commands legions of acolytes, many willful in their allegiance, but many, also, who are witless or unwary and who do not recognize death when actually confronting it."[36] He warns that there are those who "succumb to death's temptations for, so to speak, the most idealistic or earnest motives."[37] Stringfellow understands these principalities of death in terms of the devil. He notes that "ascertaining the objective existence in this world of the power of death" does not require belief "in an anthropomorphic idea of a devil with horns and a tail and a red complexion."[38] Stringfellow adds that "One does not have to be a literalist about the classical images of the devil" to know that "in this world with all of its principalities and powers, the ascendant reality, apart from the reality of God himself, is death."[39] Stringfellow also urges that the power of death is appropriately given "the name of the Devil" because of its "exceeding great power" and "presumption of sovereignty over *all* of life."[40]

Stringfellow warned that "The understanding of principalities and powers is lost nowadays in the churches, though, I observe, not so much so outside the churches."[41] On a visit to Harvard in the early sixties, Stringfellow found that students in the Business School "displayed an awareness, intelligence, and insight with respect to what principalities are and what are the issues between principalities and human beings."[42] However, on the same visit he found that students in the Divinity School mostly felt that terms such as "principalities and powers" were "archaic imagery having no reference to contemporary realities."[43] For his part, Stringfellow is clear that the "common denominator" of all "demonic claims against human life" is *dehumanization.*[44] He urges that "each and every stratagem and resort of the principalities seeks the death of the specific faculties of rational and moral comprehension which specially distinguish human beings from all other creatures."[45] This is death through total loss of identity. Stringfellow adds that "demonic aggression always aims at the immobilization or surrender or destruction of the mind and at the neutralization of abandonment or demoralization of the conscience. In the Fall, the purpose and effort of every principality is the dehumanization of human life, *categorically*."[46]

The power of death takes many specific forms, and it is evident in many particular ways. Stringfellow notes that "Men are veritably besieged, on all sides, at every moment simultaneously by these claims and strivings of the various powers, each seeking to dominate, usurp, or take a person's time, attention, abilities, effort; each grasping at life itself; each demanding idolatrous service and loyalty."[47] In many cases, the power of death is active in various levels or aspects of a particular situation. For example, with respect to racism, Stringfellow hopes that Christians will recognize the "monstrous contradiction" and corruption of racism.[48] But he expects more from the "Christian conscience about racism." Stringfellow urges that "For the Christian, it is not just that racism is morally wrong for this society but, rather, that in any of its vulgar or sophisticated forms it is a sign of death at work. Racism is one of the ways in which men and institutions suffer that separation from one another which represents their own loss of identity in the Fall."[49] Stringfellow realizes that the advocates against social evil are not immune from the power and deceptions of death. He notes that death "is occupied in the civil rights movement luring some to behold integration as an idol."[50]

Stringfellow also found the power of death at work in the professions through "internal indoctrinations focused on conforming practitioners and external publicity propagated about the various professions."[51] Recalling his own experiences in training, Stringfellow considers "the legal profession specifically, and the professions and disciplines and occupations in general" as "among the fallen principalities and powers engaged (regardless of apparently benign guises and pretenses) in coercing, stifling, captivating, intimidating, and otherwise victimizing human beings." In terms of the working of death through dehumanization within a profession, Stringfellow adds that the "demand for conformity in a profession commonly signifies a threat of death."[52]

With respect to the war in Vietnam, Stringfellow and Towne wrote to the Berrigan brothers in federal prison that "in America now, the war itself, the reality of fear, the temptation to silence, the contempt for reason, the paralysis of conscience—all of these, and more—are in truth ways in which death itself is enshrined as the moral purpose of society, as an idol."[53] Similarly, Stringfellow notes that in America "there has been no more blunt, no more terrible apparition of the moral reality of death domineering the nation than the war in Indochina."[54] However, Stringfellow warns that "this Indochina war did not sponsor the moral power of death in American society." On the contrary, Stringfellow urges that the war "expresses, grotesquely, the moral presence of death which has always been in America, as in other principalities. And the end of the war promises no end, no diminishment even, to *that* presence."[55] Stringfellow was a political dissenter and advocate for social justice, but he was also a theologian with keen skill for identifying the many threats and faces of death.

Stringfellow was more than a voice for social reform. He believed that abuses such as militarism, bigotry, and governmental intimidation were symptoms of a deeper problem in the United States and elsewhere—the pervasiveness of the powers of death, and the human tendency to worship and be corrupted by those powers. Speaking theologically, he understood this situation as the Fall. The Fall means that "all of creation exists in bondage to death, without any power to prevail against death."[56] He was clear that it would take more than an end to desegregation and the war in Vietnam to reverse the Fall. In many ways, Stringfellow pointed to the victory of life over death as the only real victory.

THE WILDERNESS EXPERIENCE: HELP FOR THE HELPLESS

Stringfellow points to a paradox concerning the human encounter with death: the person is helpless in the face of death, but there is help available in the condition of human helplessness. The temptation in the face of death is to *avoid* helplessness, but that results in human grasping for security or power or diversion in a way that does not help. Such grasping amounts to seeking the protection of an idol, which is reverence for death as the ultimate source of human meaning and the ultimate arbiter of human affairs. In this way, the person who grasps to avoid helplessness will predictably be drawn deeper into bondage to the power of death. Instead, the person facing death must first admit and embrace the condition of helplessness. This will involve a letting go of idols, and it can be a moment of conversion. Stringfellow explains that "Conversion is the event during which a person finds himself radically and absolutely helpless. In becoming a Christian, a person sees that he is naked, exposed, and transparent in every respect—he is completely vulnerable."[57] In that moment of emptiness, the person can be most fully open to God. Stringfellow notes that

> To ask God in faith for the knowledge of Him that embraces the profound knowledge of self in relation to the rest of creation is to enter upon an estate of utter helplessness. Utter helplessness: it is an experience in which all is given up, in which all effort and activity of whatever sort ceases, not only in which all answers are unknown, but unattempted, and also in which all questions are inarticulated and abandoned.[58]

In the moment of utter helplessness, all schemes and idols and diversions and power plays and efforts to grasp control must be *let go*. Stringfellow adds that this moment of helplessness is "the time in the wilderness."[59]

The gospel story of Jesus' temptation in the wilderness is a cornerstone for Stringfellow's theology. He discusses Jesus' "wilderness interlude" in *Free in Obedience, Instead of Death*, and *Count It All Joy*.[60] He explains in *Count It All Joy* "That the *only* temptation at all, for any man, at any time, is to succumb to the idolatry of death is disclosed and enacted decisively in the episode of Jesus in the wilderness (Matthew 4:1-11; cf. Mark 1:2-13; Luke 4:1-13)."[61] The wilderness is the place of emptiness and helplessness, but the wilderness is also the place of *victory*. Stringfellow notes in *Free in Obedience* that "To be in the wilderness is to be alone with the reality of one's own death, to be confronted with the reign of death in all the world. In the wilderness the power of death tempts Christ with the offer of worldly dominion, but Christ is victorious over all the claims and temptations of death."[62]

In *Instead of Death,* Stringfellow states that "To be in the wilderness represents a concrete encounter with death . . . . But the wilderness is also a place into which Christ himself has come and in which Christ has already been victorious over the claims and temptations of death."[63] Jesus' victory in the wilderness can be both example and cause for our own victory in the face of death. Relative to St. Paul, Stringfellow explains that "Paul entered the wilderness in his conversion and beheld the triumph of Christ in the wilderness; Paul went into the wilderness and was there protected from death by Christ."[64]

Christ's victory is the effective help for the helpless in the face of death. And, notwithstanding Christ's victory, the person remains in one sense helpless in the face of death. The wilderness is still the wilderness, and death is still death. Indeed, the person must remain helpless (free of grasping, free of idols) to receive God's gift of help. The person must remain vulnerable. Stringfellow notes that "one who knows justification to be a gift of the Word of God is spared no aggression of the power of death but concedes no tribute to the power of death while awaiting the vindication of the Word of God in the coming of Jesus Christ in judgment."[65] Stringfellow states that "the gift of faith involves enduring the full assault of the power of death in one's own life in relationship to the claim of death over all of life and, in the same event, suffering the power of God overcoming death in one's own existence in relation to the rest of creation."[66] Out of this encounter with death, and victory in Christ, comes "emancipation from the power of death."[67] Explaining his title in *Count It All Joy,* Stringfellow notes that Christians who share the vocation to "enjoy their emancipation from the power of death wrought by God's vitality in this world" can "count all trials as joys for, though every trial be an assault of the power of death, in every trial is God's defeat of death verified and manifested."[68] There is help for the helpless in the wilderness. There is victory in the face of death, and emancipation from its power.

ETHICS FOR AN ESCHATOLOGICAL CHRISTIAN COMMUNITY

Stringfellow's guidance for Christian living in the world has an underlying conviction: encounters with the power of death are inevitable, but Christ has won the victory over death. There is nothing we need to "do" to protect ourselves or overcome the power of death because God has already triumphed. Ironically, attempts to evade death or "single-handedly" overcome it can draw us deeper into death's bondage. Grasping for power in the face of death can substitute idols for God and turn us from receptive trust in God's gift. Stringfellow explains that the Christian "is confident that the Word of God has already gone before him. Therefore he can live and act, whatever the circumstances, without fear of or bondage to either his own death or the works of death in the world."[69]

What we do in the face of death (and what we refrain from doing) is shaped by our eschatological hope. The "occasion for praising the Word of God, in every way, in all things, is already with us. There is actually nothing else that needs to be done, and so whatever we do is transfigured into a sacrament of that praise."[70] Praise for God is at the heart of our response in faith. Our trusting receptiveness for God is enough, because "The only thing that really matters is to live in Christ instead of death."[71] We can experience the power of Jesus' victory over death in our lives today, and we anticipate the fulfillment of that victory in our lives and in the world. It is Jesus' resurrection, and not anything we do for ourselves, that is ultimately decisive.

Stringfellow notes that the victory of life over death is shared by God through the church, especially in the sacrament of baptism. He explains that "Baptism is the sacrament of the extraordinary unity among humanity wrought by God in overcoming the power and reign of death; in overcoming all that alienates, segregates, divides and destroys men in their relationships to each other, within their own persons, and in their relationship with the rest of creation."[72] The victory of life is shared corporately in the church, the community of the baptized. And the individual Christian's vocation is shaped by and rooted in membership of the faith community. In *Instead of Death*, Stringfellow urges that "the vocation of the baptized person is a simple thing: it is to live from day to day, whatever the day brings, in this extraordinary unity, in this reconciliation with all men and all things, in this knowledge that death has no more power, in this truth of the resurrection."[73]

Christ's victory of life also authorizes and empowers an active and sometimes public resistance by the Christian to the powers of death in the world. Stringfellow notes in *Free in Obedience* that the Christian "is enabled and authorized by the gift of the Holy Spirit to the Church and to himself in baptism to expose all that death has done and can do, rejoicing in the freedom of God which liberates all men, all principalities, all things from bondage to death."[74] And the freedom of emancipation from the power of death enables Christian generosity for service, sacrifice, and witness. Stringfellow states that "the Christian is free to give his own life to the world, to anybody at all, even to one who does not know about or acknowledge the gift, even to one whom the world would regard as unworthy of the gift."[75]

The Christian vocation includes generosity and active resistance to the power of death. Stringfellow explains that the drama of history "is not a conflict between evil and good, as secular ethics supposes, but concerns the power of death in this world and how death is overpowered in this life by the power of the Resurrection."[76] This victory of life over the powers of death occurs daily, in history, through the lives of Christians who also seek the fulfillment of that victory in the coming of the Kingdom of God. For Stringfellow, the Christian witness against death is rooted in an eschatological hope. He explains that "It is the juxtaposition of death and Resurrection that authorizes the Christian involvement in worldly affairs of all sorts and that verifies the eschatological hope which Christians have for all men and the whole of creation."[77]

At a personal level, Stringfellow explains, resistance to death is *humanizing*. The powers of death threaten the person with loss of identity and the seductive undermining of moral and rational faculties. The powers of death offer idols in place of hope and trust in God. But resistance to the powers of death is humanizing, and a necessary aspect of Christian life. Stringfellow notes in *An Ethic for Christians and Other Aliens in a Strange Land* that it is the crisis of personal confrontation with death "which *is* the definitively humanizing experience. Engagement in specific and incessant struggle against death's rule renders us human."[78] Simply stated, *"No* to death means *yes* to life."[79]

Stringfellow also states that confrontation of death is humanizing, "whatever the apparent outcome."[80] Political or worldly success is never the ultimate measure of Christian witness against the power of death. For example, Stringfellow points to the "hopeless" situation of those who resisted the Nazis during World War II. He notes that to calculate their actions—abetting escapes, circulating mimeographed news, hiding fugitives, obtaining money or needed documents, engaging in various forms of noncooperation with the occupying authorities—in terms of odds against the Nazi efficiency and power and violence and vindictiveness would seem to render their witness ridiculous."[81] But, Stringfellow urges, "the act of resistance to the power of death incarnate in Nazism was the only means of retaining sanity and conscience. In the circumstances of the Nazi tyranny, *resistance became the only human way to live*."[82]

Stringfellow also cites the Barmen Declaration by the confessing church in Germany that "publicly rebuked the demonic reality of political authority in the emerging Nazi state."[83] This declaration did not stop the rise of the Nazis, and it led to the execution, imprisonment, or exile of everyone who signed it. Politically, the Barmen Declaration was a failure. But it was an "exemplary witness," a confession of the lordship of Christ, and an "admonishment that the Word of God is active in judgment in this world."[84] The declaration was also for its signers an affirmation of trust in God and an expression of their humanity in the face of the power of death. There is strong biblical precedent for such a witness. In *A Simplicity of Faith,* Stringfellow urges that the Book of Acts chronicles "the many arrests, trials, imprisonments, exiles, tortures, and executions suffered by the pioneer Christians at the behest of the ruling authorities."[85] Their faithfulness to the gospel is the real issue in the confrontations with the ruling authorities—not their effectiveness or prospects of success in worldly terms. As they "speak and act faithfully in the gospel," they "exemplify in their living the truth and power of the Word of God transcending and disrupting the reign of death, and the idolatry of the power of death, in any and all regimes of this world."[86] In this regard, Stringfellow viewed the Berrigan brothers' resistance to the powers and principalities of death (resisting the war in Vietnam and, later, resisting the proliferation of nuclear weapons) as "standing squarely within the Apostolic precedent, engaged in a witness both venerable and normative, bespeaking the resurrection of Jesus."[87]

For Stringfellow, advocacy against the power of death is a responsibility of the church and an aspect of the vocation of the baptized. This is a recurrent theme in Stringfellow's theology. In *Instead of Death,* Stringfellow states that "The biblical lifestyle is *always* a witness of resistance to the *status quo* in politics, economics, and all society. It is a witness of resurrection from death."[88] And in *Conscience and Obedience,* he urges that "Advocacy is how the church puts into practice its own experience of the victory of the Word of God over the power of death, how the church lives in the efficacy of the resurrection amidst the reign of death in this world, how the church expends its life in freedom from both intimidation and enthrallment of death or any agencies of death . . . ."[89]

The church's vocation against the powers of death is eschatological, rooted in Christ's victory of life and eagerly anticipating the fulfillment of that victory in the Kingdom of God. Stringfellow explains in *Free in Obedience* that "The Church as Church, the Church living in and by the freedom bestowed in Pentecost, is the foretaste and forerunner—the priest (or representative) and prophet—of the reconciled society. The Church as Church is the image of God's own Kingdom, of the Eschaton."[90] The church pioneers the fulfilling of the Kingdom of God in the world, and that vocation directs the church's witness against the powers of death. Stringfellow states that "the vocation of the Church of Christ in the world, in political conflict and social strife, is inherently eschatological . . . . The Church is the trustee of the society which the world, now subjected to the power of death, is to be on that last day when the world is fulfilled in all things in God."[91]

The church is to be an eschatological community: people who share by baptism the victory over death of Christ's resurrection, people who share in anticipating the fulfillment of that victory in all creation and the coming of the Kingdom, people whose eschatological hope for the future leads them to witness against the principalities of death in the world today, people who share the church's vocation to incarnate and pioneer the fulfilling of the Kingdom of God in creation.

DEATH, RESURRECTION, AND THE CIRCUS

For Stringfellow, as for all Christians, resurrection and not death is to have the last word. He understood resurrection life in Christ as available to be realized now, today, in our struggles with the powers and principalities of death. He urges that resurrection "refers to the transcendence of the power of death, and of the fear or thrall of the power of death, here and now, in this life, in this world."[92] Resurrection thus concerns the fulfillment of life *"before* death."[93] Stringfellow likewise urges that, as beneficiaries of Jesus' resurrection, we are "to live here and now in a way that upholds and honors the sovereignty of the Word of God in this life in this world, and that trusts the Judgment of the Word of God in history."[94] Christ's victory of life over death is for us today. Our eschatological hope of life in Christ is to be realized in us now, in the midst of the possibilities and the threats we face today. This "means freedom *now* from all conformities to death, freedom *now* from fear of the power of death, freedom *now* to live in hope while awaiting the Judgment."[95]

The circus was for Stringfellow an ideal symbol of the realized eschatological community that embodies and reveals the present victory of life over death. He found the circus performance to be "a parable of the eschaton," in which "human beings confront the beasts of the earth and reclaim their lost dominion over other creatures."[96] Stringfellow considers the circus performer to be "the image of the eschatological person—emancipated from frailty and inhibition, exhilarant, militant, transcendent over death—neither confined nor conformed by the fear of death any more."[97] In the circus, "the risk of death is bluntly confronted and the power of death exposed and, as the ringmaster heralds, defied."[98] Stringfellow's joy in the circus and its defying of death likewise provides an insight into his motivation. The defying of death in all its guises was his passion, and the consistent focus of his many forms of ministry.

A LIFE AGAINST DEATH

Stringfellow's theology must be understood in terms of the total witness of his life. He lived in an era of political controversy and radical dissent in the United States. He certainly experienced the controversies to the full. And his experience was a *lived* experience. Stringfellow sought to resist the poverty and destruction in his neighbors' lives through his law practice in one of Harlem's poorest tenement districts. Stringfellow's public and personal support for Daniel Berrigan was pivotal. Stringfellow resisted the power of death in his body in order to address a crowd gathered for Berrigan's trial in Baltimore. He urged that the forces of death must not have dominion, meaning the variety of principalities that would dehumanize and diminish life through needless violence and intimidation of dissent. Stringfellow would not be intimidated to deny hospitality to a friend who was a fugitive of conscience, and he would not be silenced by the possibility of official reprisal. The Christian witness against death was *the* theme in Stringfellow's theology. He notes that most of his books focus "upon the death/resurrection motif."[99] In his writing and in all his life, Stringfellow identified and unmasked the guises of death in the world. He faced death directly, as he faced the theological and moral questions of his life. Daniel Berrigan remembered Stringfellow in the poem, "Death and life of a friend," a portion of which says, "Stringfellow bethought; Death lacking a name" and later adds, "We must break this thrall / once for all, became his mind's / holy obsession and vocation."[100] Stringfellow believed in the victory of life, and he eagerly anticipated its fulfillment. He called on the church to claim the victory of life over death, as he called on Christians to participate in that victory by resisting death in their world. Stringfellow was an advocate against death. That was his vocation, and witness.

NOTES

1 An earlier version of this essay appeared in the *Anglican Theological Review*.

2 Walter Wink, "A Mind Full of Surprises," in *Sojourners,* 14:11 (December 1985), 25.

3 Ibid.

4 William Stringfellow, *Instead of Death,* second edition (New York: Seabury Press, 1976), 1.

5 Jim Wallis, "A Tribute to William Stringfellow," *Sojourners* 14:4 (April 1985), 2.

6 Wink, "A Mind Full of Surprises," 25.

7 Wallis, "A Tribute to William Stringfellow," 2.

8 H. Coleman McGehee, Jr., "Empowering Spark," *Sojourners* 14:11 (December 1985), 26-27.

9 Melvin E. Schoonover, "Present and Powerful in Life and Death: William Stringfellow's Quest for Truth," *Sojourners* 14:11 (December 1985), 14.

10 William Stringfellow, A *Second Birthday* (Garden City, New York: Doubleday, 1970).

11 Anthony Towne, "On Sheltering Criminal Priests," in William Stringfellow and Anthony Towne, *Suspect Tenderness: The Ethics of the Berrigan Witness* (New York: Holt, Rinehart and Winston, 1971), 18.

12 Daniel Berrigan, *Block Island* (Greensboro, North Carolina: Unicom Press, 1985).

13 William Stringfellow, *Conscience and Obedience* (Waco, Texas: Word Books, 1977), 16.

14 Schoonover, "Present and Powerful in Life and Death," 14.

15 William Stringfellow, *The Politics of Spirituality* (Philadelphia: Westminster Press, 1984), 88.

16 William Stringfellow, *An Ethic for Christians and Other Aliens in a Strange Land* (Waco, Texas: Word Books, 1973), 85.

17 Towne, *On Sheltering Criminal Priests,* 18.

18 Thomas Merton, *The New Man* (New York: Farrar, Straus and Giroux, 1961), 3. Another parallel with Stringfellow is found in Merton's critique of militarism as a false idol and embodiment of the power of death relative to the Hiroshima bombing in "Original Child Bomb." Thomas Merton, "Original Child Bomb," *The Collected Poems of Thomas Merton* (New York: New Directions, 1977), 291-302. Merton's view of the idols of totalitarianism and militarism can

also be seen in his essays, "Christianity and Totalitarianism" and "The Root of War Is Fear." Thomas Merton, "Christianity and Totalitarianism," in *Disputed Questions* (New York: Farrar, Straus and Giroux, 1960), 127-48; Thomas Merton, "The Root of War Is Fear," in *New Seeds of Contemplation* (New York: New Directions, 1962), 112-22.

19 Stringfellow, *The Politics of Spirituality, 84.*

20 Stringfellow, A *Simplicity of Faith: My Experience in Mourning,* in the "Journeys in Faith" series, ed. Robert A. Raines (Nashville: Abingdon Press, 1982), 52.

21 Ibid., 68.

22 Ibid., 67.

23 William Stringfellow, *Count It All Joy* (Grand Rapids, Michigan: William B. Eerdmans Publishing, 1967), 52.

24 William Stringfellow, *Dissenter in a Great Society* (New York: Holt, Rinehart and Winston 1966), 136-37.

25 William Stringfellow, A *Simplicity of Faith,* 47.

26 Stringfellow, *Dissenter in a Great Society,* 137.

27. Stringfellow, *Instead of Death,* 19-20.

28 Ibid., 20.

29 Stringfellow, A *Simplicity of Faith,* 49.

30 Stringfellow, *Instead of Death,* 22.

31 Ibid.

32. Stringfellow, A *Simplicity of Faith,* 110.

33 Stringfellow, *An Ethic for Christians and Other Aliens in a Strange Land,* 69.

34 Stringfellow, *Conscience and Obedience,* 70.

35 Stringfellow, A *Simplicity of Faith,* 32.

36 Stringfellow, *Count It All Joy,* 91.

37 Ibid.

38 William Stringfellow, *Free in Obedience* (New York: Seabury Press, 1964), 69.

39 Ibid.

40 Stringfellow, *Count It All Joy,* 89.

41 Stringfellow, *Free in Obedience,* 50.

42 Ibid., 51.

43 Ibid.

44 Stringfellow, *An Ethic for Christians and Other Aliens in a Strange Land,* 97.

45 Ibid.

46 Ibid.

47 Ibid., 90.

48 Stringfellow, *Dissenter in a Great Society,* 138.

49 Ibid., 138-39.

50 Ibid., 140.

51 Stringfellow, A *Simplicity of Faith,* 127.

52 Ibid.

53 Stringfellow and Towne, *Suspect Tenderness,* 177.

54 Stringfellow, *An Ethic for Christians and Other Aliens in a Strange Land,* 70.

55 Ibid.

56 Stringfellow, *Dissenter in a Great Society,* 136.

57 Stringfellow, *Instead of Death,* 108.

58 Stringfellow, *Count It All Joy,* 47-48.

59 Ibid., 48.

60 Stringfellow, *Free in Obedience,* 35; idem, *Instead of Death,* 109-110; idem, *Count It All Joy,* 86-88.

61 Stringfellow, *Count It All Joy,* 86.

62 Stringfellow, *Free in Obedience,* 35.

63 Stringfellow, *Instead of Death*, 109-110.

64 Ibid., 110.

65 Stringfellow, *Conscience and Obedience*, 112.

66 Stringfellow, *Count It All Joy*, 52.

67 Ibid., 52, 93.

68 Ibid., 93. This is the basis for the title, *Count It All Joy*.

69 Stringfellow, *Free in Obedience*, 128.

70 Stringfellow, *The Politics of Spirituality*, 85.

71 Stringfellow, *Instead of Death*, 112. This is the basis for the title, *Instead of Death*.

72 Ibid., 111-12.

73 Ibid., 112.

74 Stringfellow, *Free in Obedience*, 128.

75 Ibid.

76 Stringfellow, *Dissenter in a Great Society*, 136.

77 Ibid.

78 Stringfellow, *An Ethic for Christians*, 138.

79 Ibid., 156.

80 Ibid., 138.

81 Ibid., 118.

82 Ibid., 119.

83 Stringfellow, *Conscience and Obedience*, 70

84 Ibid., 70-71.

85 Stringfellow, A *Simplicity of Faith*, 137.

86 Ibid.

87 Ibid. See A *Simplicity of Faith*, 134-37.

88 Stringfellow, *Instead of Death*, 100-101.

89 Stringfellow, *Conscience and Obedience*, 94-95.

90 Stringfellow, *Free in Obedience,* 103.

91 Stringfellow, *Dissenter in a Great Society,* 142.

92 Stringfellow, A *Simplicity of Faith,* 138.

93 Ibid. Stringfellow rejoiced that Anthony Towne "had *already* known the resurrection from the dead" when he died. Ibid., 140.

94 Ibid., 113.

95 Ibid.

96. Ibid., 89.

97 Ibid., 90.

98 Ibid.

99 Stringfellow, *Instead of Death,* 3.

100 Daniel Berrigan, "Death and life of a friend," *Sojourners* 14:11 (December, 1985), 29.

A RELUCTANT ANGLICAN PROPHET

JAMES E. GRIFFISS

Jewish and Christian scriptures make it clear that it is dangerous and even futile to try to domesticate a prophet. Prophets have a habit of breaking through the boundaries we would impose on them. Yet, even prophets have homes in which they live, however reluctantly, and families which affect their prophecy, however much they may quarrel with those families. Indeed, one might say that only in terms of the home and family from which he or she comes can a prophet prophesy.

Such was true, I believe, of William Stringfellow. He was certainly a prophet for social causes and a protester against much that he thought wrong in society and in the religious community. Yet he was a product of the society in which he lived. He was, indeed, in many ways a quintessential American; with all of his anger and protest against American society, he was deeply involved with it; he stayed and fought, and, as far as I know, he never thought of leaving his native home for a more congenial place. Indeed, he was quite aware that there was no more congenial place to which he could flee all of the failures of the United States.

And he was, furthermore, all of his life not only a serious, devout, and committed Christian, but also an Episcopalian—a quarrelsome yet very active member of a church which seems to many people (as it often did to him) to be a most ardent defender of the status quo and a very strange and alien home for a prophet. In spite of all his quarrels with the Episcopal Church, however, he faithfully remained with it. Therefore, I do not think it is possible to understand the prophetic Stringfellow without taking seriously his place within the Episcopal Church and the Anglican tradition of which the Episcopal Church is a part, however reluctantly he remained with it. At the risk of domesticating him, I want, in this essay, to locate him within this church which was always for him a home and family. I hope to show that, indeed, his prophetic voice was not alien to at least one dimension of Anglicanism and the Episcopal Church. Not to belabor a metaphor, but I suggest that he shared a room with some others in the same Anglican house, even while protesting against other members of the same household.

The Episcopal Church has both profited by and suffered from its ancestry in the Church of England. That ancestry, on the positive side, has given to the Episcopal Church a strong sense of having a public role within the nation; while small in size, the Episcopal Church has not acted like a sect (in Troeltsch's terms), standing apart from the nation. As a result it has always had a sense of social responsibility and participation in national affairs. On the other hand, because of a certain establishment mentality inherited from the Church of England, it has also been identified, more often than not, with the privileged and powerful in society. Even in Stringfellow's time (although that time may now have passed completely), the Episcopal Church often acted as though it were the quasi-established church within a Christian commonwealth, supporting the civil order and providing moral and spiritual guidance and justification for it.

Although this establishment mentality often meant identification with money and power, there were other times when it did not. There were times when Anglicans both in England and in the United States prophesied against both the political powers and the ecclesiastical ones. Somewhat like the Hebrew prophets of old, they have denounced priests and kings and, more recently, presidents and prime ministers.

That tradition of prophets who were raised up within the Established Church of England and the quasi-established Episcopal Church in the United States emerged most prominently in the latter half of the nineteenth century, although it had its origins much earlier in Anglican history. Richard Hooker, the sixteenth-century theologian to whom Anglicans most often look for theological encouragement, attempted to provide a foundation for the position of the Church of England over against other Christian bodies which threatened to disrupt the social order and for the justification of the religious and political establishment of the English nation. For Hooker, Anglican polity had its origin in his understanding of Jesus Christ as the incarnate presence of God in political order as well as in the more personal and religious ones. For Hooker, religion was not a private affair. The Incarnation of God in Christ provided a foundation for what he advocated as a Christian Commonwealth—the ordered relationship of human beings to God in church and state. Each had its own sphere of responsibility, but each also stood under the rule of God. The concept of England as a Christian nation did not, of course, survive for long, but it affected many of the attitudes which Anglicans have toward the political and social order. For some, it still functions as a nostalgic ideal.

In the nineteenth century, in quite different political and theological circumstances, several Anglican theologians, both in England and in the United States, recovered Hooker's understanding of the doctrine of the Incarnation, although not all of them drew the same political conclusions. Like him, however, they saw Incarnation not simply as a doctrine or teaching about Jesus Christ, but more fundamentally as a way, first, of interpreting and understanding the church and the society in which they lived and, second, as a way of transforming both. F. D. Maurice, himself something of a theological prophet in the first half of the century, began the recovery by preaching and writing and, to a certain degree, witnessing in his own life (he was involved with a college for workingmen) that to believe in the Incarnation of God in Christ had as one of its consequences the belief that the social order had to be shaped and governed by what the Incarnation reveals to us of God and of God's purpose for all human beings. For Maurice, the Incarnation, as a Maurician scholar says of him, reveals God's will that "human society . . . like human nature itself has been hallowed" and that "humanity, created in the image of the social God, is bound together in Christ, and . . . that divine justice demanded justice on earth . . . ."[1]

For us a century and a half later, such a theological teaching may not sound so radical, but in its time it was, and it began a heritage which in the next several generations led to the increasing identification of the Church of England and the American Episcopal Church with the poor, immigrants in the cities, and the labor movement. Clergy and lay people in the Church of England and in the Episcopal Church began significant work in the slums of London and New York at the end of the nineteenth century. In the early twentieth century, Anglicans in both countries openly advocated forms of Christian socialism over against the economic and social policies of the time. The Guild of St. Matthew in England, founded by Stewart Headlam, was especially important. Also in England, the movement known as Liberal Catholicism, of which Bishop Charles Gore and, later, William Temple, were the acknowledged leaders, stood for the involvement of the church in political and economic affairs. The guiding principle, which was lived out in social action of various kinds, was that Jesus Christ as the Incarnate presence of God in human history perfectly expresses God's purpose for society: that all women and men, no matter what their social and economic status are called to share in the life of God. Their ultimate calling to God should now be a mark of the political society, and the Christian community should witness to it and encourage it through the sacramental life of the church.

In the Episcopal Church in the nineteenth and early twentieth centuries, this Maurician teaching found advocates who are now almost forgotten by Episcopalians: James O. S. Huntington, William Dwight Porter Bliss, and Vida Dutton Scudder, to name only the most prominent. Huntington originally founded the monastic Order of the Holy Cross in order to work with the poor and the immigrants in New York City. Vida Scudder, a convert to the Episcopal Church as a consequence of her contacts with Maurician movements in England, wrote extensively in favor of a Christian socialism based on the

Catholic tradition in Anglicanism. She was a professor at Wellesley College until her death in 1954, but she was also actively involved with settlement work in Boston and was a close friend of Jane Addams in Chicago. Bliss, also in the tradition of Maurice, was actively involved in the emerging labor movement. While he did not share all of the more Catholic theological convictions of Huntington and Scudder, he did share their belief that the Episcopal Church could function as an instrument of change and be a sign of a society which could realize the social principles of Jesus Christ. He wrote, for example:

> In Christ God became man *on earth*. He took all Humanity into Himself. Christ was not only a man but MAN—man in his entirety, man in art, in science, in letters, in politics, in society, in commerce, and in industry. In the Incarnation all life entered into God. There is the breath of the Incarnation.[2]

These three early "radicals" and prophets differed in many ways, and they carried out their work differently. They all, however, shared a common theological conviction: that the Incarnation of God in Christ led Christians, and especially those Anglicans for whom the Incarnation was deeply important, to struggle against the injustices of the social order and to work for the identification of the church with the poor and powerless. For Huntington and Scudder, the struggle for justice was deeply nourished by the sacramental life of the church, especially the Eucharist, for it was in the worship of the church, they believed, that the incarnate presence of Christ for human society was known.

William Stringfellow also shared in this tradition. It is evident in all his writing that he believed the Incarnation and the sacraments of the church required prophetic action. Whether he was actually aware of the connection between himself and earlier Anglican prophets is not explicit in his published writings. He makes no mention, as far as I can determine, of any of them, but his convictions about the Incarnation and the sacramental life for the church and its social mission are clear.[3]

The connection is clear in his earliest writings. In the late fifties, after having graduated from Harvard Law School, Stringfellow went to work in East Harlem which was at that time experiencing an influx of people from Puerto Rico. He began to work with the East Harlem Protestant Parish as a layperson, and he practiced law among the poor. It would, I think, be true to say that his understanding of Christianity and especially of the Incarnation was shaped by his time there and by the people with whom he was involved as an advocate and friend. It was, indeed, his contact with the East Harlem Protestant Parish which gave him a particular insight into the importance of the Incarnation and, consequently, of the work of the church, not just in East Harlem, but wherever it was to be found.

The Parish had been formed by students from Union Theological Seminary. They understood their mission to be preparing the poor and disadvantaged of East Harlem to hear the Word of God through their advocacy for social change, education, improving housing, and the like. As Stringfellow says, in criticism of the Parish, the young ministers who worked there believed that only when the social issues had been resolved, "when the lives of the people were less burdened with poverty, discrimination, illiteracy, and ignorance, then the time would come to preach the Gospel and then the people, no longer so preoccupied with their afflictions, would be able to hear and embrace the Gospel."[4] Stringfellow was very critical of this point of view, not only for practical reasons—he thought that it led to a neglect of worship and the reading of the Bible. He was also critical of it because of what it said about belief in Jesus Christ. In words which echo what Bliss had said earlier, he wrote,

> . . . the Christian faith is not about some god who is an abstract presence somewhere else, but about the living presence of God here and now, in this world, in *exactly* this world, as men know it and touch it and smell it and live and work in it . . . . The meaning of Jesus Christ is that the Word of God is addressed to men, to *all* men, in the very events and relationships, any and every one of them, which constitute our existence in this world. That is the theology of the Incarnation.[5]

To illustrate his point, Stringfellow tells a story, as he so often does,[6] about a young man with whom he worked. The young man was addicted to narcotics, and, Stringfellow says,

> He is dirty, ignorant, arrogant, dishonest, unemployable, broken, unreliable, ugly, rejected, alone. And he knows it. He knows at last that he has nothing to commend himself to another human being. He has nothing to offer. There is nothing about him that permits the love of another person for him. He is unlovable. Yet it is exactly in his own confession that he does not deserve the love of another that he represents all the rest of us. For none of us is different from him in this regard. We are *all* unlovable. More than that, the action of this boy's life points beyond itself, it points to the Gospel, to God who loves us though we hate Him, who loves us though we do not satisfy His love, who loves us though we do not please Him, who loves us not for our sake but for His own sake, who loves us freely, who accepts us though we have nothing acceptable to offer Him. Hidden in the obnoxious existence of this boy is the scandalous secret of the Word of God.[7]

Stringfellow's theological point here is, of course, that the Word of God does not depend on, is not conditional on, our readiness or preparation for it. Precisely in our poverty—whether economic and social or personal and individual—God's Word in Christ comes to human beings. The Incarnation means that God is present now; the church's work is to make that presence known, not to make God present. This presence of the Word of God is the foundation for the church's social and political advocacy, not the other way around.

The name, as he calls it, "Word of God," is an important and rich one in all of Stringfellow's theological and political writings, and what he means by it illustrates his profound incarnationalism. In a later book, *Conscience and Obedience*, in which he develops a political theology based on Romans 13 and Revelation 13, he makes clear that "Word of God" ties together the relationship between God and the world, a relationship which he was always concerned to develop. He says that for him "the Word of God" refers not only to the Bible as the Word of God, but also to the Word incarnate in Jesus Christ, the Word active in the world as the Holy Spirit, and the Word present in the whole of creation.[8]

In an earlier book, *A Private and Public Faith*, when he was actively involved with the East Harlem Parish, Stringfellow also began to develop a sacramental theology which gave expression to his radical understanding of the presence of the Incarnate Christ in the church. What he says there reflects his unhappiness with the Parish itself.

> In Jesus Christ there is no chasm between God and the world . . . . The reconciliation of God and the world in Jesus Christ means that in Christ there is a radical and integral relationship of all men and of all things. *In Him all things are held together* (Colossians 1:17b).
>
> The Church as the Body of Christ in the world has, shares, manifests, and represents that same radical integrity. All who are in Christ—each member of His Body in the world—know and live in the same integrity in his relationships with any creature in his own, specific personal history. Existentially and empirically, the reconciliation of the world with God in Jesus Christ establishes a man in unity with both God and the whole world. The singular life of the Christ is a sacrament—a recall, a representation, an enactment, a communication—of that given actual unity, whether in the gathering of the worshipping congregation now and then or whether in the scattering of the members within the daily affairs of the world . . . . The Body of Christ lives in the world in the unity between God and the world wrought in Christ and, in a sense, the Body of Christ lives in the world *as* the unity of God and the world in Christ . . . . [W]hen a congregation gathers in sacramental worship, the members of the Body are offering the world to God, not for His sake, not for their own sake, but for the sake of the world, and the members then and there celebrate God's presence in the world, and on behalf of the world, even though that world does not yet discern His presence.[9]

And later he writes,

> The experience of being a Christian is one of continually encountering in the ordinary and everyday events of life the same Word of God which is announced and heard, remembered and dramatized, expected and fulfilled in the sanctuary of the Church. To celebrate the Word of God in the sacramental worship of a congregation is an anticipation of the discernment of the same Word of God in the common life of the world. To be in the presence of the Word of God while in the world authenticates the practice of sacramental life within the congregation. One confirms and is

confirmed by the other. In each place, in both world and Church, the Word is the same Word, and, in each place, in both practical life and sacramental life, the response elicited and the task required of the Christian is the same.[10]

This linking together of Incarnation, sacramental worship, and the involvement of the church and of individual Christians in the politics of the world was also a dominant theme in the Anglican "radicals" of the last century both in England and in the United States. Stewart Headlam in England and Vida Scudder in the U.S., whom I have already referred to, saw the Eucharist, especially, as a political act. For them it was a sign both of the hoped-for unity of all human beings in political society (what they called "socialism") and of the responsibility of the Christian community to work for a society which did not differentiate among human beings because of economic and political power.[11]

Stringfellow develops his ideas of the political importance of worship and the sacraments in another early book, *Dissenter in a Great Society*. There he writes about liturgy as a political event: "At no point in the witness of the Church to the world is its integrity as a reconciled society more radical and more cogent than in the liturgy, the precedent and consummation of that service which the Church of Christ and the members of this Body render to the world."[12] He is careful to point out that liturgy is not something "spooky" or magical and mechanistic. Rather, whether it is elaborate or simple, liturgy is "a dramatic form of the ethical witness of Christians in this world," so long as it is characterized by certain definite marks.

What Stringfellow says about liturgy here is written against the background of his experience with the East Harlem Parish, where he had been unhappy with the lack of attention to worship. While he does not identify himself as an Episcopalian in what he has to say, he is quite obviously drawing on the tradition of Anglican worship and sacramental theology. Indeed, his comments anticipate much that would later become standard teaching among Anglican liturgists. It should be remembered that during the sixties, the Episcopal Church was beginning the process of revising the Book of Common Prayer, and liturgists were focusing on a greater sense of the liturgy of the

Eucharist as a communal act and on worship itself as involvement with the everyday world of the worshipers. There was also an increasing emphasis on the reading of Holy Scripture and the importance of preaching at every act of public worship. In the sixties there was much turbulence about such changes, but much that Stringfellow says here was incorporated into the Prayer Book of 1979.

First, he calls for scriptural integrity: "relating the ubiquity of the Word of God in history to the consummation of the Word of God in Jesus Christ . . . . A biblically authentic and historically relevant liturgy is always the celebration of the death and Resurrection of the Lord . . . ."[13] Consequently, he argues, in order for liturgy to have integrity there must be both preaching and liturgy, word and sacrament.

Second, liturgy is both a transcendent and present event. It celebrates reconciliation as God's act remembered and hoped for and the reconciliation of the gathered community in a particular time and place. As such, it commits Christian people to their life in the world: "All authentic witness in the name of Christ, exemplifying in the world the virtue of Christ, which Christians undertake in their dispersion in the practical life of the world, is portrayed in the liturgy celebrated in the gathered congregation." The liturgy is also a sacrament:

> Sacramentally, we have in the liturgy a meal which is basically a real meal and which nourishes those who partake of it as a meal. At the same time, this meal portrays for the rest of the world an image of the Last Supper, of which Christ Himself was Host, and is also a foretaste of the eschatological banquet in which Christ is finally recognized as the Host of all men.[14]

The sacrament of the liturgy is a political event and a social act, when it acts out the Gospel. Then, it characterizes the nature and calling of the life of the Christian in the world.

> Worship which has integrity in the Gospel is always an intercession by God's people for the cares and needs of the world, and always a thanksgiving—a eucharist—for God's love for the world. Worship at the altar is thus authenticated by the constant involvement of the people of the Church in the world's life and by the public witness of the Church in the world.[15]

Finally, in what is surely a reflection of the heritage of F. D. Maurice and Vida Scudder, he writes:

The Christian political witness, for the individual Christian and for the body of the Church, means demonstrating in and to the world what the true society is by the living example of the society of the Church.

The Christian political witness is affirming and loving the essential humanity of all in Christ in the midst of men's abdication of human life and despite the whole array of death's assaults against human life.

The Christian political witness is the audacity to trust that God's love for this world's existence is redeeming, so Christians are human beings free to live in this world by grace in all practical matters and decisions.

That is why the Church of Christ is the only society in this world worthily named great.[16]

Had Stringfellow only developed an incarnational and sacramental theology for the church and the world, he would simply have had an honored place among many other Episcopalians who did much the same thing: a somewhat critical theologian of a quasi-established church which was able to live in relative comfort with the Constantinian settlement. However, Stringfellow cannot be so easily domesticated. He pushed beyond the borders and became a rebel not only within the church but also within the political society. Stringfellow saw something about the Incarnation which his Anglican forebears did not articulate quite so clearly: the destructive power of the institutions and ideologies of the created order of world and church and the obligation of Christians to fight against their power.

Another Anglican theologian, who was an Archbishop of Canterbury, anticipated Stringfellow's prophetic challenge to Christians, although in a much more restrained voice. In 1939, at the beginning of World War II, Archbishop William Temple, certainly a leading exponent of an incarnational theology and an inheritor himself of the Maurician tradition, said that a new task lay before Christian theology in the new situation of England and the world. He called for a new direction in incarnational theology:

> [O]ur task with this world is not to explain it but to convert it. Its need can be met, not by the discovery of its own immanent principle in signal manifestation through Jesus Christ, but only by the shattering impact upon its self-sufficiency and arrogance of the Son of God, crucified, risen and ascended, pouring forth that explosive and disruptive energy which is the Holy Ghost. He is the source of fellowship, and all true fellowship comes from him. But in order to fashion true fellowship in such a world as this, and out of such men and women as we are, He must first break up those fellowships with which we have been deluding ourselves. Christ said that the effect of His coming would be to set much at variance. We must expect the movement of His spirit among us to produce sharper divisions as well as deeper unity.[17]

Stringfellow was certainly one of those who could have appreciated the importance of Temple's words, especially when the Archbishop spoke of breaking up the fellowships with which we have been deluding ourselves. Stringfellow saw those fellowships as the principalities of which St. Paul wrote, and he even went so far as to speak of them as demonic and as the power of the antichrist in a fallen world.

There are many areas in which this can be seen. In his work as an attorney before his illness, Stringfellow radically engaged himself with the poor and outcast of society, and consequently his writings always reflect the disturbing presence of those who are alienated from church and society. His radical stance over against both church and society arose out of his taking seriously—that is, "hearing"—the voices of the "others," those who were themselves aliens in American society and for whom the church had little to offer. Because he heard those alien voices, Stringfellow was deeply conscious of "the dangerous memory of Jesus" (Johannes Metz) and the divisions which that memory caused for a society which liked to call itself "Christian."

His own experience with illness and the death of his companion and friend Anthony Towne made him conscious of the theological importance of both. Death became for him a metaphor of the alienation of society and of the power of the principalities of this world.[18] And, while he denied that he was a "Barthian," he certainly reflected the theology of Karl Barth in his recognition of the radical transformation which the Cross requires of human beings for their redemption.[19]

However, his most profound movement beyond the Anglican incarnational tradition of accommodation between church and society is expressed in his support of Daniel Berrigan and the Catonsville Nine during the opposition to the American war in Vietnam. He extended hospitality to Berrigan, and he and Towne were indicted for "harboring a fugitive," although subsequently acquitted.[20] Those actions, and others associated with it, were a defiance against the established order, both political and ecclesiastical, and it forced him to become profoundly aware of what he called the principalities and powers in regard to which he saw himself as a *Christian* alien.

Stringfellow had always been critical of government and its various follies and stupidities. As he wrote in 1964:

> From the point of view of Christian faith, the monstrous American heresy is to think that the whole saga of history takes place merely between a celestial God and terrestrial men. But the truth is quite otherwise, both Biblically and empirically: The drama of history takes place among God, men, *and* the principalities and powers, those dominant institutions and ideologies active in this world . . . .[21]

In another book published in the same year, *Free in Obedience,*[22] he analyzed the biblical and contemporary meaning of principalities and powers, identifying them as those institutions and ideologies which claim dominion over human beings by denying and denouncing the sovereignty of God.

It was, however, in 1973, that he most systematically (at least for him, since Stringfellow was not a "systematic" theologian!) reflected on the relationship between Incarnation and the status of being an alien in a world dominated by the principalities. The book, which is a political reflection on the book of Revelation, was appropriately titled, *An Ethic for Christians and Other Aliens in a Strange Land.*[23] In it he made a sustained analysis of what are the principalities against which the Christian must struggle, not simply as an individual, but as part of a community of believers in Christ.

"Principalities" are all institutions, from the most mundane and innocent to the most complex and powerful, because all human institutions participate in the Fall and can become powers for death:

> The principalities are numbered among God's creatures, yet they suffer the Fall as truly as human beings, as truly as the rest of Creation. It is not that there are no perfect or perfectible institutions (though there are none), but rather that all institutions exist, in time, in a moral state which is the equivalent of death or which has the meaning of death.[24]

In other words, Stringfellow resisted any attempt to sacrilize institutions, especially any attempt to do so by those who called themselves Christians. And yet he also recognized that the "principalities" are themselves part of creation and, therefore, ultimately under the Lordship of the Incarnate Christ. Christians, above all others, ought to be able to recognize and to battle against all institutions, whether of church or state. Because they are Christians, they know both the power of the Fall and the hope of the redemption of all things, including the principalities, in Christ. The work of the church, which itself is one of the principalities because it, too, is an institution within fallen creation, is to struggle always to be "a new nation, incarnating and sacramentalizing human life in society freed from bondage to the power of death."[25]

This recognition, indeed, proclamation, of the theological significance of the Fall as an event which governs the whole creation is the defining characteristic of Stringfellow's theology. And it sets him off from much of the Anglicanism in which he otherwise found a home. It sets him apart from the Anglican tendency to treat the Incarnation as simply a "yes" to the world, without at the same time uttering a "no" to the demonic forces which can and do dominate it as a consequence of the Fall—what Archbishop Temple meant when he spoke of our desire to understand the Incarnation to explain, and even to justify, the world in which Christ has become incarnate, rather than to convert it.

Stringfellow was not "anti-church." Quite the contrary, he wrote that all individual prophetic actions taken by Christians are not individualistic. They are actions of the Body:

> There is no unilateral, private, insulated, lonely, or eccentric Christian life. There is only the Christian as the member of the whole body; the Christian vocation for every single Christian is inherently ecumenical; the exclusive context of biblical ethics is biblical politics; even when a Christian acts apparently alone he

does so as a surrogate for the Church; baptism signifies the public commitment of a person to humanity.[26]

"A Christian," Stringfellow wrote, "says no to the power of death but in the same breath he bespeaks the authority of life freed from bondage to death." The Christian affirms

> the aspiration for new life intuitive in all human beings and inherent in all principalities. He confounds the wiles and stratagems of death by insistently, defiantly, resiliently living as no less and none other than a human being . . . . He warns of the autonomy of God's judgment while rejoicing in the finality of God's mercy. He suffers whatever death can do as he celebrates the resurrection from death here and now. [27]

Stringfellow's no and yes, Fall and Redemption, remains a prophetic voice which the Christian church, and especially the Episcopal Church, always needs to hear. In the end, Incarnation and the redemption of creation is God's and our final yes, but God's no to all of the principalities stands as the sign of God's judgment and, therefore, as a prophetic witness to all of us that we, too, are aliens who live in a fallen world.

> Christ's resurrection is for human beings and for the whole of creation, including the principalities of this world. Through the encounters between Christ and the principalities and between Christ and death, the power of death is exhausted. The reign of death and, within that, the pretensions to sovereignty over history of the principalities is brought to an end in Christ's resurrection . . . . In the same event in which the pretension of the principality is exposed and undone, how and in whom salvation is wrought is disclosed and demonstrated. In Christ the false lords of history, the principalities, are shown to be false; at the same time, in Christ the true Lord of history is made known. In Christ is both the end and fulfillment for all principalities, for all humanity, and for all things.[28]

And Stringfellow, the alien and reluctant prophet, did know where, finally, he was at home:

> It is categorically impossible to profess the Christian faith in separation or isolation from the Church as it is in its empirical reality. It is not a possibility to be a Christian and to renounce Christendom even though it be part of the vocation of a Christian to attack Christendom, for thus may the Church be renewed."[29]

NOTES

1 John Orens, "Politics and the Kingdom: The Legacy of the Anglican Left," in Paul Elmen, ed., *The Anglican Moral Choice* (Wilton, Connecticut: Morehouse-Barlow, 1983), 65.

2 W. D. P. Bliss, *What is Christian Socialism?* quoted in Bernard Kent Markwell, *The Anglican Left: Radical Social Reformers in the Church of England and the Protestant Episcopal Church, 1846-1954* (Brooklyn, New York: Carlson Publishing, 1991), 119. Markwell's study provides a thorough analysis not only of Bliss, but also of Huntington and Scudder, and traces their indebtedness to F. D. Maurice and the later tradition of Christian socialism in the Church of England, especially the Guild of St. Matthew.

3 I am told by Bill Wylie-Kellermann that Stringfellow's library was dispersed after his death, so that it is not possible to know from that source what books he read and studied.

4 William Stringfellow, *My People Is the Enemy* (New York: Holt, Rinehart and Winston, 1964), 86.

5 Ibid., 97. This passage is also quoted in Bill Wylie-Kellermann, *A Keeper of the Word: Selected Writings of William Stringfellow* (Grand Rapids, Michigan: William B. Eerdmans Publishing, 1994), 140. Because Stringfellow's books are now out of print and hard to come across, this judicious collection is invaluable for the study of Stringfellow. Whenever I quote a passage which is also quoted by Wylie-Kellermann, I shall give the citation in his collection (hereafter W-K). I have not, however, altered Stringfellow's use of masculine references, although I quite agree with W-K's decision to do so in his much more lengthy selections.

6 William Stringfellow, *A Simplicity of Faith* (Nashville: Abingdon Press, 1982), 20. Stringfellow says that biography—"any biography and every biography"—is theological because it is incarnational; it shows "how the living Word of God is implicated in the actual life of this world . . . ."

7 Stringfellow, *My People Is the Enemy*, 97-98.

8 William Stringfellow, *Conscience and Obedience* (Waco, Texas: Word Books, 1977), 14. Cf. W-K, 10, 24, 313.

9 William Stringfellow, *A Private and Public Faith* (Grand Rapids, Michigan: William B. Eerdmans Publishing, 1962), 40-41. See W-K, 164.

10 Ibid., 57.

11 In addition to Orens and Markwell, for an analysis of the importance of the Socialist movement and the sacraments, see William L. Sachs, *The Transformation of Anglicanism: From State Church to Global Communion* (Cambridge: Cambridge University Press, 1993), chapter 6.

12 William Stringfellow, *Dissenter in a Great Society* (New York: Holt, Rinehart and Winston, 1966), 150 ff. This discussion can be found in W-K, 123-126.

13 Ibid., 151.

14 Ibid., 153-54.

15 Ibid., 159-60.

16 Ibid., 163-64.

17 Quoted in Arthur Michael Ramsey, *An Era in Anglican Theology: From Gore to Temple* (New York: Charles Scribner's Sons, 1960), 160-61. Ramsey himself pointed to some of the limitations of Anglican incarnational theology, as it was developed by Gore and others, earlier in this study. See 27-29.

18 See, for example, Robert Boak Slocum, "William Stringfellow and the Christian Witness against Death," *Anglican Theological Review* 77:2 (Spring 1995), 173-86.

19 See, for example, his conversation with Karl Barth in W-K, 187-191, and other references.

20 See W-K, 85-86, for "A Statement by the Accused," a statement by Stringfellow and Towne in response to the indictment.

21 Stringfellow, *My People Is the Enemy*, 147.

22 William Stringfellow, *Free in Obedience* (New York: Seabury Press, 1964). See W-K, 192-203.

23 William Stringfellow, *An Ethic for Christians and Other Aliens in a Strange Land* (Waco, Texas: Word Books, 1973).

24 Ibid., 80; W-K, 20ff.

25 Ibid., 58.

26 Ibid., 61.

27 Ibid., 63-64.

28 Stringfellow, *Free in Obedience*, 73; W-K, 203.

29 William Stringfellow, "On Being a Reluctant Episcopalian," unpublished manuscript courtesy of Bill Wylie-Kellermann.

WHAT'S A NICE EVANGELICAL BOY LIKE YOU DOING READING A BOOK LIKE THAT?

JEFFREY A. MACKEY

The introduction came during the first semester of my senior year of college. Collateral reading for a course in Christian ethics included a book by a William Stringfellow with the title, *An Ethic for Christians and Other Aliens in a Strange Land.* I was captivated by the title and chose to report on the work based solely on this intrigue. The book, no doubt, would not have made a required reading list at my college—it was a small, conservatively evangelical college just a few miles north of New York City on the west bank of the Hudson River—but this particular professor, Don J. Kenyon, was a bit of a maverick. "Try Stringfellow. He will stretch you, Jeffrey," was his comment. And so I did. And so I was.

The reading of the book—or, should I say, the *first* reading of the book—happened quickly. I could not release it. I read it in its entirety as rapidly as I could. I returned, re-read, and devoured every page, every paragraph, every word. I marked the book so often that, by semester's end, it was necessary to replace my worn out volume. I wrote my report, and, as I remember, the grade was a good one. But then, look at the subject matter I held in my hand!

But the question which followed me into the pastorate on graduation was, "What is a nice evangelical boy like you doing reading a book like that?" It was not written by the typical "evangelical" authors—it had none of the authority of the "big names" we had encountered in other courses; it was published by a popular publishing house and not a scholarly press; and the fact that the author was an Episcopalian would particularly make him suspect. But providentially, the book was allowed. I took the choice, and it became my assignment. I was taken by Stringfellow that semester—grabbed as no author had ever grabbed me, moved in ways I could not *then* and can scarcely *now* fully expound. I found a person outside the scope of our narrow conservatism who commended himself to me, and to this wise professor, by his commitment to the Word of God.

I did not then, nor for many years afterward, endeavor to investigate the compelling reasons for my love affair with the writings of William Stringfellow. I knew I liked what he wrote, how he wrote it, and how I was continually challenged by it. Over the years I have sought out all the books he wrote and copied all the periodical articles I could find, and as I have moved from ministry in my small evangelical denomination into the priesthood in the Episcopal Church in my fortieth year, I reintroduced myself to William Stringfellow.

This time my approach was one of self-examination. Why did I read this man in the first place? What was it about him that captivated me at such an early age? Why could I embrace his ideas when he was so far outside the circles in which I lived and moved? What was it? I must discover the draw he had for me (and as I would learn, for many other evangelicals as well).

We evangelicals were nothing if not committed to the Word of God. Our doctrinal statements lifted the written word to levels of "inerrancy" and "infallibility" in the original autographs. And suddenly I read this writer, Stringfellow, who, without pledging loyalty to these terms, honored and esteemed the Word of God in ways far beyond those of major theologians of my theological persuasion, or of any theological persuasion I was familiar with. He indicated in his writings the need to read the Word of God; that the Word of God was active, alive; that it possessed a power and an energy which was present in it, waiting for its own self to be met with belief and claimed in commitment. He writes,

> The Word of God is for men . . . . The Bible has not merely rele-
> vance, but, much more than that, a present vitality as the Word of
> God for men in these times.[1]

I was impressed with his use of the Bible: in his home, in his
church, in gatherings of friends, and as the raw material for his writing and speaking. (And he would certainly agree that this Word of
God was "raw material"—nothing pablum-like here!) He saw a manifest versatility in the Word of God—it somehow survived and flour-
ished in spite of realities arrayed against it.

> The Word of God persists in fallen creation—inherent or residual,
> hidden or secreted, latent or discreet, mysterious and essential (cf.
> Romans 1:20; James 1:21). Having the eyes to behold that pres-
> ence of the Word, or having the ears to listen to the Word, having
> the gift of discernment, is, indeed, the most significant way in
> which Christians are distinguished from other human beings in
> this world.[2]

This was impressive to this young ministerial student. That a layman, and an Episcopalian at that, would so honor scripture, and
beyond scripture, the Word of God, that it was the source for everything he wrote about, was basically unheard of. We had been taught
that "the liberal wing of the church" doesn't take the Word of God
seriously. They play with words, redefining them and denying them."
And all of a sudden, here was Stringfellow affirming them, proclaiming them, and giving them immense and deep definition. He saw the
synthesis of truth which we were so fiercely endeavoring to guard in
our evangelical naiveté. His statements placed him firmly in the camp
of one honoring the Word of God:

> The revelation of the Word of God is, always, more manifold and
> more versatile than human comprehension. What I anticipate in
> the passages is not consistency so much as coherence. I can live
> and act as a biblical person without the former, but without the lat-
> ter I cannot live . . . . I look for style not stereotype, for precedent,
> not model, for parable, not proposition, for analogue not aphorism,
> for paradox, not syllogism, for signs, not statutes. The encounter
> with the biblical witness is empirical, as distinguished from
> scholastic, and it is confessional, rather than literalistic, in either
> case, it, over and above any other consideration, involves the com-

mon reader in affirming the historicity of the Word of God throughout the present age, in the biblical era and imminently.[3]

It must be that this primal commitment to the Word of God by Stringfellow was one of my major attractions to him. His use of the term and concept of "historicity" took a great hold, in light of the demythologization and spiritualizing movements which had so threatened anything historical in the Word of God. As one looks back over Stringfellow's works, the panoramic view is that his willingness to see the Word of God historically as well as empirically is the point of his strength. He expected that the Word of God was living and active—and his expectations were actualized.

Not that this historic commitment made him credulous—not at all. He is clear that

> I am not one, however, inclined toward using the conditioning of history to explain discrepancy or incongruity in the Bible. At the same time, I harbor no compulsion to neatly harmonize Scripture . . . . The whole notion that the Bible must be homogenized or rendered consistent is a common academic imposition upon the bible literature but it ends often in an attempt to idealize the Bible in a manner which denies the most elementary truth of the biblical witness, namely that it bespeaks the dynamic and viable participation of the Word of God in the common events of the world. The militant character of the Word of God in history refutes any canon of mere consistency in the biblical witness. To read the Bible is to hear of and behold events in which the Word of God is concerned, attended by the particularity and, to human beings, the ambiguity of actual happenings. Any efforts to read the Bible as a treatise abstractly constructed or conformed usurp the genius of the Bible as testament of the Word of God active in history. If the biblical witness were internally strictly consonant, after the mode of ideology or philosophy, the mystery of revelation in this world would be abolished; revelation itself would be categorically precluded.

> What is to be expected, instead of simplistic consistency, in listening to the Bible, allowing for the vagaries and other limitations of human insights, is coherence: a basic integrity of the Word of God or the fidelity of the personality of God to his creation.[4]

Certainly closely tied with this focus in Stringfellow was his use of and honor for the Bible itself. He told people to handle it, use it, read it. Many of his Bible studies were begun and many continued with the reading of the Bible with little or no comment. It was this Bible focus which involved, or prepared and enabled the Christian to be involved in the real world.

> A spontaneous, intimate, and incessant involvement in the biblical Word as such—that is, Bible study—is the most essential nurture of contemporary biblical people while they are involved, patiently and resiliently, in the common affairs of the world.[5]

Whether he was instructing teens in a Sunday school or sitting at his kitchen table, Stringfellow's respect for, and honor of the Bible set him starkly aside from his mainline heritage (and from much of evangelicalism, I might add). The impression on my young conservative mind was nothing less than remarkable, and I read on. He took the Bible seriously and caused me to wrestle with its images and to grapple with its teachings.

But not only did Stringfellow honor and employ the Word of God and the Bible, he elevated the biblical concept of prophecy to a contemporary reality which jettisoned the shallow interpretations given to it by the growing charismatic element in American Christianity. Commenting on the charismatic movement as such, he indicts and prescribes in one broad stroke of the pen:

> . . . discernment is the elementary, common, and ecumenical gift, intrinsic to the authority which every Christian receives, essential to the efficient use of all other charismatic gifts, characteristic of the mature Christian witness in the present day no less than long ago.[6]

He indicted the modern shallowness of interpretation and definition of prophecy by claiming that it lacked "boldness."

> It is not that church people are too proud, but that they are not bold enough; it is not even very pertinent to this issue that American Christians are apostate, since what is more relevant is that they are adolescent in biblical faith.[7]

Prophecy for Stringfellow was in essence a forth telling of truth in such a way as to address the contemporary scene with the relevance and integrity of the Word of God. That intrigued me. Later, he would do the same with the concept of "sanctification." Whereas prophecy was a new act of the Christian mind, sanctification was a new act of the Christian life.

> ... *sanctification is a reiteration of the act of creation in the Word of God.* Thus sanctification refers to the activity of the historic Word of God renewing human life (and all of created life) in the midst of the era of the fall, or during the present darkness, in which the power of death apparently reigns.[8]

This placed Stringfellow precisely where the evangelical community believed itself to be but somehow could not arrive: indicting society in which it lived and moved, and correcting it with the Word of God (in prophetic voice) and in model (sanctification).

That Stringfellow defined his terms was particularly appealing since the academic circles in which I found myself had long over-used and under-developed definitions of terms which had become somewhat meaningless. The frustration I often faced with worn-out definition was met with renewed insight and freshness in the depths of meaning which Stringfellow found in each biblical concept. His definitions did not always square with what I had been taught, and I was sent often to the scriptures themselves to research the meanings of words which I had tossed around with pseudo-authority. I was suddenly and powerfully given the meanings of the words Stringfellow had so discerningly discovered. Whereas the evangelical writings (many of them excellent theological treatises) in which I was steeped had often narrowly defined terms, or left them undefined, opting rather for individualistic meanings, and whereas the "liberal" theological climate had redefined words so as to deny the power of many of them, Stringfellow seemed universally to define his terms biblically, and found their meaning and purpose[9] in what was meant by the biblical writers.

> I eschew games with proof-texts. The biblical Word is worthy of a better attention than manipulative verbal gamesmanship, however piously motivated.[10]

He does not second-guess the biblical authors:

> There comes a moment when words must either become incarnated or the words, even if literally true, are rendered false.[11]

He showed me how to incarnate the words of the Word.

Many years after my initial contact with his writings, I read the account of his reluctantly teaching a high school Sunday school class by reading and rereading the Book of Romans. The goal was to hear the Word of God. He withheld interpretation for the benefit of revelation and illumination. That was a powerful statement to this young pastor/theologian.

My undergraduate experience was completed within the years of the Vietnam War. Stringfellow could not have been more relevant. In our particular denomination, the goal was to secure a "4D" deferment, go to Bible college, and become a pastor as soon as possible. The "Great Commission"[12] demanded this. I followed that pathway. Taking a conscientious objection stand with the United States never would have entered my mind. Our theology had grown somewhat out of the eighteenth-century millenarian theologies, and America was God's nation to do God's bidding. Whereas Stringfellow covered his car with bumper stickers proclaiming "Question Authority," our campus sported cars with stickers such as "America: Right or Wrong."

Now into my theological milieu comes the lay theologian declaring that Christianity demands an anarchical stand against the "principalities and powers" masquerading as the government of the United States (or any other nation for that matter).[13]

I had never conceived of Christianity and politics being related. It had not dawned on the mind of this twenty-one-year-old that Christianity had anything to say about the political enterprise. But Stringfellow addressed politics with the Word of God. He told his readers that the Word of God was pertinent to the political, institutional, and governmental powers of my own day. This I could not immediately accept, having been indoctrinated with the individualistic gospel of American evangelicalism, but his arguments were compelling, and I eventually began to grasp the depth and breadth of his meaning. Soon I found that *An Ethic for Christians and Other Aliens in a Strange Land* did indeed address the contrarieties I was beginning to sense between my own evangelical convictions and the "strange land" in which I was being called to minister. Soon I would be graduated from Bible college and would be taking my first pastorate. The demands would increase. I needed an answer to the often sung rhetorical question, *"Is this vile world a friend to grace to help us on to God?"* And in Stringfellow I found the poetical question placed squarely within the prose of applicable theology. My first personal realization of this "principality and power" nature was with the denominational institution. Soon I saw it applicable in the national government as the scandal of Watergate loomed large on the horizon of our country's politics and ethics.

With this addressing of the political scene by the Word of God, I was drawn to investigate Stringfellow further. All of this was brought about by my being taken with his predicating of his theology on the acceptation and reality of the Fall. Writing in the preface of his most popular book, Stringfellow says

> Contending as I do that Americans are, in a rudimentary way, biblically illiterate and that the radical moral confusion within the nation stems from that illiteracy, it is possible to state my concern in different words, and blatantly: *most Americans are grossly naïve or remarkably misinformed about the Fall.* Even within the American churchly environment, there prevails too mean, too trivial, too narrow, too gullible a view of the biblical doctrine and description of the Fall. Especially within the churches there is a discounting of how the reality of fallenness . . . afflicts the whole of Creation, not human beings alone but also the principalities, the nations included.[14]

This naiveté about the Fall was precisely in its limited definition. It so often excluded anything apart from the individual human being. Again, he writes

> American pietism—both in the social gospel and in evangelicalism—is entranced with a notion that the Fall means the consequences of mere human sin, without significant reference to the fallen estate of the rest of Creation.[15]

He called his readers to understand the immense pervasiveness of the Fall, affecting and afflicting all of Creation, humanity, principalities, and all. If this is true, it would answer many of the questions with which Western Society in the sixties and seventies wrestled. America, and especially evangelicals of the sixites and seventies had, by and large, jettisoned any relationship of the Bible to the political, rendering it apolitical. The pietism of the past had shaped doctrines and ethics of these decades, declaring ethics and spirituality as one, and rendering each radically individualistic.

This, too, Stringfellow addressed.[16] Though it would take many years for me to come to a full understanding of his teaching, I read with interest, and marked profusely throughout the section of the book where he deals with the corporate ethic, or the ethic of the body as it regards the church. Not to be missed is his pronouncement based firmly on biblical teaching, that

> There is no unilateral, private, insulated, lonely, or eccentric Christian life. There is only the Christian as a member of the whole body; the Christian vocation for every single Christian is inherently ecumenical; the exclusive context of biblical ethics is biblical politics; even when a Christian acts apparently alone he does so as a surrogate for the Church; baptism signifies the public commitment of a person to humanity.[17]

Christ is Lord of history and time and, as such, reigns over everyone and everything, not only me.[18] Thus, Stringfellow saw the biblical Christ as the historic and empirical Christ.

The historic Christ encountered people (plural) and this was precisely the vitality of his message. Stringfellow was saddened that Christ is "demeaned to become a nebulous, illusive, spiritualized figure, a sacred vagueness severed from his own historic ministry."[19] Only a conviction which places Christ again as Lord of history will save us from such a flaccid Christ.

This was and is deeply moving, challenging, and appealing to many. There was nothing of the demythologizing of scripture, though this was popular at the time. What it said, it said. Wrestle with what is there—don't explain it away. There was no differentiation between the Christ of faith and the Jesus of history. As a matter of fact, he writes interestingly enough, "Among Americans, especially church folk, there is probably a greater need to demythologize the Antichrist than to demythologize Christ."[20] It was, for Stringfellow, fundamentally due to its "mundane history" that the Bible yields up ethics and virtues, which are the stuff of authentic Christian living. And since this is true, believers are then thrust back into time and history where principalities, powers, and salvation all move simultaneously.

That he would marry together the books of Romans and Revelation (as he does in *Conscience and Obedience*) initially was an anomaly to me. Soon the mists rose and I saw the interrelatedness of doctrine and life. It was this exact point which fundamentalism missed and for which evangelicalism was frantically grasping. I began to see that Stringfellow might be the bridge between evangelicalism and mainline Christianity (and to this day, I believe this to be the case, though he is not yet realized as such).

All of this lay firmly at the foundation of Stringfellow's convictions and teachings about the Word of God and the Bible. Certainly this was impressive to my evangelical mind (and obviously to others, as history bears out). But there were obviously other appealing things about this man and his lay theologies.

That he took seriously the gifts of the Spirit and the reality of the demonic is most arresting. He could seriously see the demonic without charismatizing it.[21] With the rise of the charismatic movement within American Christendom, there was a frantic race to find demons everywhere, and to beat others in being the first to cast them out. Stringfellow had nothing to do with such nonsense. Demonism was the natural consequence of the Fall. The biblical description of the Fall concerns the "alienation of the whole Creation from God" and thus the rupture and profound disorientation of all relationships within the whole Creation. This was too simple; yet it made enormous sense as I contemplated the often asinine rovings of deliverance workers I encountered. "Legion" was his name for the principalities and powers of the world.[22] He makes his point successfully, and his interpretation of the biblical witness relative to evil and the demonic is insightful. Though a little red man with a pointed tail and a pitchfork seldom enters the mind of a thinking Christian, the nebulous nature of many doctrines of the devil are displaced and made the healthier by the explicit teaching Stringfellow brings from the Bible itself.

This led to the most shaking realization which I found in his book: that institutions are creatures; creatures which have "their own existence, personality, and mode of life."[23]

I read this, re-read it, and returned again and again. Had I learned this truth early, it would have saved me two decades of frustration; but I did grasp it, though I confess that I was one of those Stringfellow called "reluctant to acknowledge" this reality.[24]

The consequences of this are both far reaching and clarifying. One is helped in understanding those groups of people and why they do what they do. In subsequent years, I was sent searching for the writings of Reinhold Niebuhr and Jacques Ellul, each of whom wrote in the same vein as Stringfellow when addressing the morality of man and the immorality of society.

Finally, one is moved by Stringfellow's acceptance of the need for and reality of evangelism.[25] Though much of what he says is delineated from later writings, I picked up on his call that biblical living "has certain characteristics and definite capacities."[26] It called for the gift of discernment, and provided the means whereby one could live within the era of the Fall. That the Christian is different goes without saying; but not in the sense of lists of do-and-don't, lists of right and wrong. Rather, the Christian life is different because it consists in giftedness—spiritual giftedness in the midst of the Fall and its chaos. Consequently, based upon this giftedness, Stringfellow would call upon believers to

> Know the Word, teach the Word, nurture the Word, preach the Word, defend the Word, incarnate the Word, do the Word, live the Word.[27]

And so, challenged by his commitment to the Word of God, and following all the implications of that commitment, this "evangelical boy" grew reading Stringfellow, moved into convictions by his clarity and challenge, and today teaches and preaches, predicated on the foundations he established.

NOTES

1 William Stringfellow, *Free in Obedience: The Radical Christian Life* (New York: Seabury Press, 1964), 7-8.

2 William Stringfellow, *Conscience and Obedience: The Politics of Romans 13 and Revelation 13 in Light of the Second Coming* (Waco, Texas: Word Books, 1977), 36

3 Stringfellow, *Conscience and Obedience,* 11.

4 Ibid., 10-11.

5 William Stringfellow, *An Ethic for Christians and Other Aliens in a Strange Land,* (Waco, Texas: Word Books, 1973), 151.

6 Ibid., 141.

7 Ibid.

8 William Stringfellow, *The Politics of Spirituality* (Philadelphia: Westminster Press, 1984), 30.

9 For example see ibid., 16-18.

10 Stringfellow, *An Ethic for Christians and Other Aliens in a Strange Land,* 42.

11 Ibid., 21.

12 Matthew 28:19-20.

13 William Stringfellow, *A Simplicity of Faith: My Experience in Mourning* (Nashville, Abingdon Press: 1982), 103ff.

14 Stringfellow, *An Ethic for Christians and Other Aliens in a Strange Land,* 19.

15 Ibid., 76.

16 See ibid., final chapter, to follow the entire argument.

17 Ibid., 61.

18 Ibid., 36.

19 Ibid., 43.

20 Ibid., 111.

21 Ibid., 139ff.

22 Ibid., 78.

23 Ibid., 79.

24 Ibid., 79.

25 See especially William Stringfellow, *Instead of Death*, (New York: Seabury Press, 1963).

26 Stringfellow, *An Ethic for Christians and Other Aliens in a Strange Land,* 138.

27 Ibid., 143.

LIVING UNDER AND
ABOVE THE LAW

JACQUELINE SCHMITT

"The milieu of the powers and principalities," William Stringfellow wrote, "*is* chaos."[1]

Stringfellow's voice was one of the ones I heard break through the chaos of the late sixties and seventies, my formative years as a student, young adult, and Christian. His appeal was in his courage, his directness, his tenacity to an uncompromising Gospel of the victory of life over the powers of death. Now, rereading several of his works years later, I am struck by the consistency of his theology and the power his words still have to cut through the chaos of this current time.

Two of Stringfellow's repeated themes stood out to me during this rereading. His theological understanding of the powers and principalities is one. A second is the tension of living, at the same time, under the law and above the law. Although the experiences which shaped the development of these themes are those of a generation or two ago, Stringfellow remains a theologian who helps us interpret the concerns and struggles of the present day and the present church.

As he wrote about the powers and principalities, Stringfellow made clear that among the institutions and ideologies held in thrall to the demonic is the church, even, perhaps especially, the church. To a college student (as I was) in the early seventies, the church seemed a refuge from the obviously wicked powers and principalities of the state, the military and the corporation. I began to think of pursuing ordination, at the time not yet approved for women in the Episcopal Church. My college chaplain was a woman seeking ordination. I became more deeply involved in the political struggle within the Episcopal Church to ordain women.

As the years, and the meetings, went on, however, the deep flaws in the character and structure of the Episcopal Church revealed themselves, most clearly and painfully in the words and actions of bishops and other church leaders. No doubt my perception of the church was colored by my own situation: I was a college student in Washington, D.C., during the years at the of the end of the Vietnam War, during the Nixon administration, the Watergate scandals, and the impeachment hearings. When bishops preached patience and caution, when they repeatedly spoke of their pain at not being able to ordain women called and qualified to be priests, I heard the same moral bankruptcy. The survival of the institutional church was held more dearly than what we perceived was the compelling truth of the gospel. When confronted with this challenge of women called to the priesthood, the Episcopal Church seemed more interested in its own decorum, its own survival. It created God in its own image, an exclusively male God, claiming the masculinity of Jesus more important to the Incarnation than Jesus' humanity. The faithful were told to wait, that the church would come around in due time.

Some ten years earlier, Stringfellow wrote this about principalities as institutions:

> The institutional principalities also make claims upon human beings for idolatrous commitment in that the moral principle that governs any institution—a great corporation, a government agency, an ecclesiastical organization, a union, utility, or university—is its own survival. Everything else must finally be sacrificed to the cause of preserving the institution, and it is demanded of everyone who lives within its sphere of influence—officers, executives, employees, members, customers, and students—that they commit themselves to the service of that end, the survival of the institution . . . . In the end, the claim for service that an institution makes upon human beings is an invitation to surrender their lives in order that the institution be preserved and prosper. It is an invitation to bondage.[2]

Church leaders not only had feet of clay, their entire beings seemed fraught with deception and spinelessness. Was this the institution into which we were demanding admission?

The trial of the Rev. William Wendt in 1975 crystallized the issue. Wendt, Rector of the Church of St. Stephen and the Incarnation in Washington, D.C., was charged with disobeying the godly admonition of his bishop by inviting a woman to celebrate the Eucharist in his parish. She had been ordained in the irregular ordination in Philadelphia in 1974. William Stringfellow was Wendt's counsel at the trial, and subpoenaed Presiding Bishop John Allin as a witness. Allin never appeared, was held in contempt of court, and never answered those charges, either. Some years later, Stringfellow addressed this issue in an open letter to the Presiding Bishop, printed in *The Witness* magazine:

> . . . in violation of your canonical duty you defied the subpoena of the court to appear and testify, and were thereupon duly adjudged in contempt of that court. You have done nothing to purge yourself of that contempt.

> There are those who refer to you as a "conservative," but that is hyperbole. Such disrespect for the law of the church as you have shown and encouraged is not a conservative trait.[3]

In a way, Allin's behavior, as interpreted by Stringfellow, saved the church for me. Clearly revealed as a principality more concerned with its own survival than even its own laws, much less with issues of justice and the gospel, the church, I began to see, held out no salvation for me, could claim no ultimate allegiance. I could hope to be free to work within it, and yet to be free from bondage to it. It became an institution that did not have to be taken as seriously as the reality to which it pointed: the kingdom of heaven, the household of God, the reign of righteousness and mercy and justice.

Stringfellow's theology gave words to deep passions. Some of the causes he espoused a generation ago have come to fruition: the Vietnam War ended, civil rights legislation was enacted, the nuclear threat abated with the end of the Cold War, women were ordained as deacons, priests, and bishops, even elected President of the House of Deputies of the Episcopal Church. Yet those are incomplete victories.

Whatever good Stringfellow achieved as a poverty lawyer working in East Harlem would today be dwarfed by the "three strikes and you're out" drive to send his young clients to prison and by the recently passed bill to "end welfare as we know it." The power of the state to intrude into citizens' lives increases. The U.S. military, although shrunk somewhat, continues to enter into armed combat around the world. The church is as deeply polarized, and as concerned with its own survival, as ever. Stringfellow made this point in 1973, writing about the Vietnam War:

> The principalities have great resilience; the death game which they play continues, adapting its means of dominating human beings to the sole morality which governs all demonic powers so long as they exist—survival. . . . This is one reason why, of course, this war has been more a symptom than a cause of the American social crisis. It is why, also, whenever the war can be said to have ended, no essential change will have been wrought in the nation.[4]

The temptation in rereading Stringfellow in these latter days is to apply his words and solutions like band-aids to the struggles we face today. The easy route for us would be to copy his thoughts, to repeat his resistances, to echo his slogans. Stringfellow has already done the hard work of discernment. He has prayed, he has worked, he has waited for the Word of God to be revealed in and through the struggles he lived. What we must now do, however, is resist the temptation to romanticize what we read and remember of Stringfellow and the times and struggles we shared with him. To follow his example of godly living in these days is to engage in the work with which he was engaged: how does a faithful Christian live under the law and above the law at the same time? How does a faithful Christian live deeply concerned with this world—with the powers and principalities which we inhabit and which surround us—and at the same time live in obedience to the God of life who creates and redeems us?

To be in and yet not of the world is a trait Stringfellow came to understand from his reading of the Bible, from his deep and life-long encounter with the Word of God. Stringfellow saw all relationships, all activities, all deeds through the brilliant prism of the light of Christ. Christ's encounter and victory over death came not once only on the day of resurrection. This victory over death so permeates the world, Stringfellow wrote, that we no longer need fear the mere deaths that the powers and principalities continue to deal to the world.

> [Christ's] power over death is effective not just at the terminal point of a person's life but throughout one's life, during *this* life in *this* world, right now. This power is effective in the times and places in the daily lives of human beings when they are so gravely and relentlessly assailed by the claims of principalities for an idolatry which, in spite of all disguises, really surrenders to death as the reigning presence in the world. His resurrection means the possibility of living in this life, in the very midst of death's works, safe and free from death.[5]

If we are to follow Stringfellow, then, doing for ourselves and in our situation the work, prayer, and discernment he did, then this awareness that we are in but not of the world must be the lens through which we see what is going on around us. New powers and principalities have been added to those named by Stringfellow but their characteristics remain as death-dealing as ever. Living in these institutions, such as church, corporation, academy, family, political party, we can be seduced into believing that their survival is worth our souls and bodies, that their ends justify our means. Even our cherished institutions and beliefs should be subjected to this scrutiny. For example, let us ask some hard questions regarding the changes in the church following the admission of women to the ordained ministry. Can we answer the charges Stringfellow leveled against the professional clergy in 1962?

> The clergy have become the hired spokesmen for religion among men. They have been invited to decorate public life, but restrained from intervening significantly in it . . . . The clergy have become the face of the Church in the world; they have become a superficial, symbolic, ceremonial laity . . . . Candidates for seminary admission . . . have been induced to think of the ordained ministry as a profession and specialty, like social work or medicine or law. They are expected only, though sometimes necessarily, to have an academic interest in the Christian faith. And there has been much emphasis upon the amenities of the "profession of the ministry," that is, clergy salaries and pensions and household allowances and long vacations and social status and the like.

> Some seminarians think and some seminary faculty assume that
> ordination, rather than baptism, is the seal of the Christian life—
> providing for those who have it the assurance and security that
> they are indeed Christians.[6]

The vocation of the Christian begins at baptism; each of us is called to follow Christ's example of giving all of our lives for the life of the world. To participate in a church whose work is any other than that, Stringfellow would say, is to participate in a church that is a principality, held in thrall to the fear of death and a desperate struggle for its own survival. How we measure up to those biblical standards is a mark of our faith. Don't merely follow me, Stringfellow would say; read the Bible and encounter the Word of God for yourself.

What, then, about Christian stewardship? What of our inherited wealth, our beautiful buildings, our secure pensions? Many parishes and dioceses these days are seeking methods for church growth and new member ministry. Other non-parochial ministries, such as the campus ministry where I am chaplain, work constantly to raise money, to build endowments, to repair buildings, to put on nice parties to convince rich people to give their money to us. Moreover, we in the Episcopal Church often pride ourselves on being the spiritual home of the powerful in business, industry, and government. That raises a very real question: what is the character of ministry with the wealthy in our pews? How do we preach the gospel to the well-meaning, the charity-oriented comfortable who benefit from the status quo and who endow our churches and pay our salaries? Stringfellow told the story of a clergyman in a wealthy parish who called him for advice for a woman about to be evicted from her apartment. "Well, sell one of your tapestries and pay the rent," he told the priest.

The churches in America have many possessions, tapestries and otherwise, which they can have and hold with integrity in any Christian sense only insofar as they are free to give them up for the world as a witness to the ministry of Christ, as a sign of dying in Christ, as an honoring of the Word of God.

> When the Church has the freedom itself to be poor among the
> poor, it will know how to use what riches it has. When the Church
> has that freedom, it will know also how to minister among the
> rich and powerful. When the Church has that freedom, it will be

a missionary people again in all the world. When the Church has the freedom to go out into the world with merely the Gospel to offer the world, then it will know how to use whatever else it has—money and talent and buildings and tapestries and power in politics—as sacraments of its gift of its own life to the world, as tokens of the ministry of Christ.[7]

There was more to Stringfellow's life than work. We can follow him through play and humor as well. His appreciation of being in but not of the world also came from his love of the circus, the realm of the clown, the holy fool. The circus celebrates the reality that things are not always what they seem. The humor of the clown comes from paradox, surprise, the inversion of power and weakness, the contrast of sublime and tawdry. The circus performer lives in the world, with all its struggles and limitations, and yet is able to soar above it, laugh at it, expose the fear of death for its shallowness in the face of the joy and grace of a life fully lived.

> . . . in the circus, humans are represented as freed from consign-ment to death. There one person walks a wire fifty feet above the ground, another stands upside down on a forefinger, another jug-gles a dozen incongruous objects simultaneously, another hangs in the air by the heels, one upholds twelve in a human pyramid, another is shot from a cannon. The circus performer is the image of the eschatological person—emancipated from frailty and inhi-bition, exhilarant, militant, transcendent over death—neither con-fined nor conformed by the fear of death any more.[8]

In the end, of course, the metaphor for Stringfellow's own life is that of circus performer. He lived in this world, as a lawyer and a Christian, with a deep ferociousness. Through his own experiences of pain and weakness, he knew the limitations and losses of mortality. Like the trapeze artist, he would follow the laws of gravity and tran-scend them at once, by letting go of the swing, risking all that he was and all that he had, secure in the knowledge that the arms that would catch him gave life and joy and hope to the world.

To reread William Stringfellow these days is to encounter a remarkable soul, who continues to support us in our struggles to con-front the powers and principalities which corrupt God's creation, to live life under and above the law, to be in the world but not of it, to risk losing our lives so that we might gain life, to live in obedience to the Word of God so that we might be free.

NOTES

1 William Stringfellow, *An Ethic for Christians and Other Aliens in a Strange Land* (Waco, Texas: Word Books, 1973), 94, quoted in Wylie-Kellermann, ed., *A Keeper of the Word: Selected Writings of William Stringfellow* (Grand Rapids, Michigan: William B. Eerdmans Publishing, 1994), 213.

2 William Stringfellow, *Free in Obedience* (New York: Seabury Press, 1964), quoted in Wylie-Kellermann, *A Keeper of the Word: Selected Writings of William Stringfellow,* 196-97.

3 Wylie-Kellermann, *A Keeper of the Word: Selected Writings of William Stringfellow,* 281.

4 Stringfellow, *An Ethic for Christians and Other Aliens in a Strange Land,* 93, quoted in Wylie-Kellermann, *A Keeper of the Word: Selected Writings of William Stringfellow,* 212.

5 Stringfellow, *Free in Obedience,* 72, quoted in Wylie-Kellermann, *A Keeper of the Word: Selected Writings of William Stringfellow,* 202.

6 William Stringfellow, *A Private and Public Faith,* (Grand Rapids, Michigan: William B. Eerdmans Publishing, 1962), 50.

7 Ibid., 86-87.

8 William Stringfellow, *A Simplicity of Faith: My Experience in Mouning* (Nashville: Abingdon. Press, 1982), quoted in Wylie-Kellermann, *A Keeper of the Word,* 353-54.

WILLIAM STRINGFELLOW
AND THE AMERICAN
RACIAL CRISIS

GARDINER H. SHATTUCK, JR.

Let it be realized that the real recalcitrant in the American racial crisis is not the so called die-hard segregationist of the South . . . . The real recalcitrants—who are very many and very important— are the nice, white liberals in the North and in the South. They include multitudes of church members. They are respectable, sane, sincere, benevolent, earnest folk. They do not despise or hate Negroes, but they also do not know that paternalism and condescension are forms of alienation as much as enmity . . . . And it is that mentality—which most white Americans suffer— which must be exorcised if there is to be reconciliation between black men and white men in America.[1]

At the end of the summer of 1956, a few months after his graduation from Harvard Law School, William Stringfellow moved to New York City to serve as the legal counsel of the East Harlem Protestant Parish. Invited by the senior professional staff of the organization, he came to assist the poor Hispanic and African-American residents of Harlem who were so often the victims of racial and social injustice. The Parish itself had been started in 1948 by a group of young clergy distressed at American Christianity's rapidly growing conformity to middle-class secular values—the phenomenon

Episcopal theologian Gibson Winter called the "suburban captivity of the churches." Stringfellow and his colleagues were also part of a larger, post-World War II movement of white religious activists seeking both to "reclaim the city" for Protestantism and to keep alive the social gospel their denominations had practiced earlier in the century. Within a few years of its founding, the Parish encompassed not only 160 communicants but also several hundred other neighborhood residents to whom it ministered in practical, as well as spiritual, ways.[2]

As one member of the Parish argued, Jesus manifested his divine calling both by preaching about heaven and by healing the bodies of the poor of his day. Although Stringfellow agreed with this basic pastoral thrust, he gradually became disenchanted with his fellow workers' lack of interest in the Bible and theological thought, as well as with the clericalism that was ingrained in the group. He was renowned for his commitment to Bible study, and he lamented the failure of other leaders in the Parish to understand the high value he placed on worship and preaching. "It's not merely that you're not taking the Bible seriously. You're not taking *God* seriously," he blurted out one day. Frustrated by his inability to effect a change, Stringfellow resigned from his position at the Parish early in 1958. However, he continued to live and work on his own in East Harlem until 1962, when he and two friends formed a law partnership in midtown Manhattan. In the early sixties, he also began to pursue his interest in bringing theological reflection to bear on contemporary social issues, each year delivering scores of lectures, most of them highly critical of the bourgeois pretensions of institutional Christianity in the United States.[3]

Stringfellow's initial ministry in Harlem coincided, of course, with the emergence of national awareness about the civil rights movement in the South. When he arrived in New York in 1956, the bus boycott in Montgomery, Alabama, was entering its final stages. The boycott, which historians now regard as a watershed in the civil rights struggle, was the first black-led protest to receive significant media coverage. A year later, the school crisis in Little Rock, Arkansas, also captured widespread attention and revealed the determination of African Americans to desegregate public education in the South. By the end of the decade, a group of liberal leaders within the Episcopal Church recognized that their denomination had been slow in supporting social changes taking place throughout the country. At a conference in December 1959, they helped create the Episcopal Society for Cultural and Racial Unity (ESCRU), an organization that was to press for racial integration both in the church and in society as a whole. Stringfellow served on a committee that planned the formation of the society, and he was involved in early debates about the strategy it was to pursue.[4]

For the first year and a half of ESCRU's existence, its leadership concentrated more on issuing statements supporting the initiatives of others in the civil rights struggle (the student "sit-ins" of 1960, for example) than on engaging personally in direct action. This emphasis changed dramatically in the summer of 1961, however, when twenty-eight priests announced that they would undertake an interracial "prayer pilgrimage" from New Orleans to Detroit, where the sixtieth General Convention of the Episcopal Church was to be held. Like the "freedom riders" of the same period, the ESCRU prayer pilgrims planned to challenge segregation laws and racial customs during the course of their journey northward. The prayer pilgrimage was only two days old when, on September 13, fifteen of the group were arrested as they entered the bus terminal in Jackson, Mississippi. Stringfellow assisted the prayer pilgrims' legal defense and eventually saw them exonerated in court.[5]

Stringfellow wrote about the prayer pilgrims a few months after the trial and drew a clear theological lesson from their experiences in Mississippi. Although he was pleased to see the priests set free, he emphasized that they owed their primary allegiance, not to the American judicial system, but to the Christian gospel, which represented a "radical affront" to the way white Americans ordinarily behaved. Even if there were no civil rights movement, he noted, all white Christians ought to "love and honor their solidarity with all other . . . baptized people," including those whom southern racial laws intended them to despise. Since baptism restores the unity of God's creation, believers are joined in Christ across racial lines. Thus, if all American Church members truly upheld their baptismal vows, there would be no need to engage in the legal confrontations that occurred in Jackson, for racism would already have been overcome.[6]

As Stringfellow's commentary on the prayer pilgrimage reveals, his attitude toward the civil rights movement was shaped not only by his political views, but also by his belief that Christianity was by its very nature relevant to the everyday world. Admired by Karl Barth, he was selected to be part of the entourage of intellectuals who accompanied the Swiss theologian during his visit to the United States in 1962, and he took Barth on a tour of Harlem to help him understand the racial crisis there. Stringfellow in turn applied Barth's ideas about the presence of God's Word in human history to the social ills they observed in American cities. The problem with most church-goers, he thought, was their tendency to divorce politics from spirituality and to imagine that God was only an abstraction. The doctrine of the Incarnation, on the other hand, demonstrated God's real-life immersion in the world. God worked both within the sanctuaries of the institutional Church and in public affairs; religious faith, therefore, had to inform a person's views on race relations and on every controversy that troubled human society.[7]

Stringfellow's involvement with ESCRU and his commitment to the civil rights cause continued through the mid-sixties. In January 1963, he was one of ESCRU's official representatives at the National Conference on Religion and Race, convened in Chicago under the auspices of the National Council of Churches, the National Catholic Welfare Conference, and the Synagogue Council of America to commemorate the centennial of the Emancipation Proclamation. The meeting brought nearly seven hundred delegates together in the first major ecumenical effort to examine the role of religious institutions in American race relations. At its close, the Conference issued an "Appeal to the Conscience of the American People," which acknowledged racism as the country's "most serious domestic evil" and called upon Christians and Jews to work for racial justice.[8]

Although Stringfellow was not one of the featured speakers at the Conference, he did rise on one notable occasion to express his displeasure with the agenda of the meeting. For white religious leaders to come together and simply issue one more statement of concern was "absurd," he said, when African Americans in northern cities were already displaying "a spirit of radical hostility and of revenge" toward mainstream society. Despite the good intentions of the many white men and women who had assembled in Chicago, the initiative in racial matters no longer rested in their hands; it belonged instead to African Americans like James Baldwin and Malcolm X, militants whom the organizers of the Conference had made no effort to contact. And even though African-American leaders such as Benjamin E. Mays and Martin Luther King, Jr., had been placed in prominent positions at the meeting, "Uncle Tom" (Stringfellow observed a few months later) had really been the most popular black person there. The whole affair, he declared, both at the Conference and on numerous occasions thereafter, had just been "too little, too late, and too lily white."[9]

In the aftermath of the National Conference on Religion and Race, leaders of the various mainline denominations seemed to heed Stringfellow's criticism. Although King's "Letter from Birmingham Jail" excoriated white clergy (including the two Episcopal bishops of Alabama) for their continuing intransigence and failure to comprehend the moral urgency of the civil rights movement, Presiding Bishop Arthur Lichtenberger responded positively on behalf of his denomination. In a pastoral letter issued in May 1963, Lichtenberger summoned Episcopalians both to pray for an end to racial discrimination and to take appropriate political action to ensure that African Americans received their constitutional rights. The Episcopal House of Bishops, moreover, meeting just prior to the August 1963 March on Washington, stated that participation in the event was both "a proper expression of Christian witness and obedience" and a means by which Christians could exercise "responsible discipleship."[10]

By this time, Stringfellow himself had gained widespread recognition as a social activist with an acute theological mind, publishing four books and numerous articles between 1962 and 1964. Stringfellow also remained in the limelight, because at the same moment when bishops were first giving serious attention to the civil rights movement in the South, he started to compare the general estrangement between the races in the North to the legalized segregation that existed in the southern states. He described, for example, the bigotry African Americans faced in New York when they tried to live outside of Harlem, and he lamented the apathy of the white community in not combating discrimination. Stringfellow accused church people of being no better than anyone else in this regard, for many small congregations closed their doors and left neighborhoods to which African Americans moved, while large, wealthy parishes tolerated occasional black visitors but never encouraged them to become communicants. He also warned (prophetically, as it turned out) that the poverty from which black people suffered in urban areas in the North made a major explosion of violence even more likely to occur there than in Mississippi or Alabama.[11]

Stringfellow and ESCRU together kept racial matters high on the list of priorities for the Episcopal Church at the 1964 General Convention, which assembled in St. Louis a few weeks before the national presidential election. Barry Goldwater (himself an Episcopalian) was known to have the backing of arch-segregationists and right-wing extremists, and political liberals like Stringfellow not only were outspoken in their opposition to his candidacy but also argued that his election as President might entirely reverse the progress of the civil rights movement. With the backing of ESCRU director John Morris, Stringfellow released "A Statement of Conscience on Racism in the Presidential Campaign" at a news conference during the Convention. This statement, which condemned Goldwater's "transparent exploitation of racism among white citizens" and accused him of "inheriting the votes of white racists," invited other Episcopalians to join in expressing their displeasure with the Republican candidate's views. Approximately eight hundred Episcopal clergy and laity eventually signed the document.[12]

Although Stringfellow in no way implied that he was speaking for the Episcopal Church as a whole, reports from the national press suggested that his statement was an official pronouncement of the General Convention. Protest against the denomination's apparent meddling in political affairs was so immediate and sharp that the House of Deputies formed a special committee to investigate the matter. The committee returned with a resolution deploring the "confusion and embarrassment" Stringfellow's actions had caused and affirming the Church's strict neutrality on candidates for political office. Despite this censure and the severe criticism he received, Stringfellow expressed satisfaction that he had accomplished his mission and succeeded in calling attention to the implicit racism in the rhetoric of the Goldwater campaign. Morris and the ESCRU membership agreed with him, and a few weeks later, the society helped raise money to reimburse Stringfellow for the expenses he incurred while attending the convention.[13]

To most liberal, white Americans, Lyndon Johnson's landslide victory in the 1964 election, coupled with the passage of the Civil Rights Act and the Voting Rights Act in Congress, appeared to herald the approaching end of racial prejudice in the United States. African-American leaders, on the other hand, recognized that the campaign against racism had hardly begun. While the securing of basic constitutional rights had been the principal focus of the civil rights movement prior to 1965, economic inequality was another form of injustice also needing to be addressed. As Martin Luther King, Jr., observed at the March on Washington in 1963, the majority of black people still lived "on a lonely island of poverty in the midst of a vast ocean of material prosperity." Despite President Johnson's declaration of "an unconditional war on poverty," debates about jobs, housing, and the reallocation of national financial resources affected a wider and far more intractable segment of the American population than had been touched by the initial stages of the civil rights movement. And when the Watts section of Los Angeles burst into flames in August 1965, the limitations of mere political reform lay exposed. Although segregation laws had been abolished and African-American voting rights had been secured in the South, the deep-rooted "culture of poverty" that some said existed in urban areas in the North seemed just as immutable as ever.[14]

In this period Stringfellow, too, began to shift his approach to racial matters, reminding white Americans of the further work at hand. For example, when throngs of white religious leaders marched from Selma to Montgomery with African Americans in Alabama, Stringfellow asked if it were truly the dramatic turning point most of them thought it was. He reminded them that African Americans needed to buy decent homes in the North as well as cast ballots in the South. The heady feeling of success inspired by the Selma march should foster more than self-satisfaction, he thought; it ought also to provide an impetus for "the momentous, undramatic, traumatic and arduous task of reconstructing society." He gave the same advice to fellow ESCRU member and seminarian Jonathan Daniels, who wrote him from Selma to say how much Stringfellow's writings had inspired his own civil rights activism. Stringfellow thanked Daniels but reminded him that his most important witness for racial harmony would probably be back home among his fellow students at the theological school in Cambridge.[15]

At the same time, Stringfellow worried that the participation of so many church people in the Selma march signified the church's return to "a simplistic social gospel," the shallow understanding of the Christian faith that was a key factor in his resignation from the East Harlem Protestant Parish a few years before. He feared that liberal religious reformers might so sacralize the secular order that they completely lost sight of the church's true eschatological character. He argued instead that the posture of the church toward the world always ought to be one of *dissent* from the prevailing status quo. Neither the "familiar, conventional, and prosperous bureaucracy" that middle-class Americans tended to call "church," nor the secular social movement that activists had transformed into a "parachurch," should be confused with the actual church of Jesus Christ. Furthermore, racism and the immense economic gap between the classes in the United States would be overcome only when white Americans renounced their "primitive and pagan ethic . . . of greed" and accepted the ethic of human interdependence enunciated in the Christian gospel.[16]

The summer of 1966 marked a critical transition for Stringfellow and other white activists. Although the civil rights movement had reached a crossroads the year before at Selma, its future became clear during the "Meredith march" in Mississippi, when militants introduced the call for "Black Power." The immediate popularity of the Black Power idea among young African Americans meant that the successful interracial alliance of black moderates, black radicals, and white liberals, first formed during the Montgomery bus boycott in 1956, was in fact about to dissolve. Soon, white leaders sensitive to black aspirations felt the need to back away from the racial struggle and let African Americans run their own affairs. Meanwhile, the escalating conflict in Vietnam, which had already drained funds away from the vaunted Great Society program and the domestic war on poverty, became the focus of widespread media attention as well. Following a trip to Vietnam early in 1966, Stringfellow also turned his energies to the expanding protest movement against the war. And by the end of the year, his work on a book about the James Pike heresy controversy and the serious deterioration of his health further curtailed his commitment to other causes. Although he spoke out briefly in 1969 in support of the Black Manifesto, Stringfellow's civil rights activism—and the activism of the majority of white Americans concerned about the racial crisis—ended effectively in 1966.[17]

As the foregoing narrative illustrates, William Stringfellow was one of many dedicated white activists who participated in and strongly supported the civil rights movement from the Montgomery bus boycott of 1956 through the advent of Black Power in 1966. Stringfellow's most remarkable contributions included, first, his immersion in the problems of the urban poor as a lawyer living in Harlem and, later, his advocacy of social change as a theologian and writer. The idealism and commitment to racial justice he demonstrated throughout that period are unquestionable. However, despite his desire to eradicate racial prejudice in society at large, he unwittingly perpetuated aspects of American racism within the Episcopal Church and, thus, partially undermined the cause he espoused. And while he clearly wished to identify himself with the ordinary men and women he knew in Harlem, some of his statements about their leaders—the few recognized leaders African Americans possessed at that time—unnecessarily denigrated the advances they were making on behalf of black people.

Stringfellow was prone, for instance, to articulate the kinds of racial stereotypes prevalent among liberal white males of his generation, dismissing African-American politicians as "Uncle Toms" and evoking the proverbial image of the otherworldly, "pie-in-the-sky" black preacher. He voiced cultural theories then popularized by white social scientists, who characterized African-American institutions as "pathological" (in Gunnar Myrdal's words) and lamented the alleged passivity of black Christians. Ostensibly escapist, otherworldly, and weakened by inadequately trained clergy, black churches seemed to encapsulate what white intellectuals thought were the worst aspects of the larger African-American community. Thus, as Stringfellow argued in 1962, the "frivolousness and irrelevance in the Negro churches and sects" made them (along with "the urban churches of white society") all but useless in the struggle for racial justice to which secular-minded activists were committed. Freedom-loving African Americans, he asserted, should no longer "be appeased by gospels which locate God out of this world nor by . . . assurances of extravagant blessings on some later day."[18]

In spite of his general concern for the plight of African Americans in a racist society, Stringfellow did not fully understand either the role black churches were playing in the civil rights movement or their importance as social centers in the black community, especially in the South. This is most clearly revealed in his reaction to a 1962 report published in *The Episcopalian*. Responding to the attention the civil rights movement had started to receive in the national news media, the editors of the church magazine decided to highlight (albeit belatedly) the ministries of a number of key black Episcopalians, including Absalom Jones, Tollie Caution (Executive Secretary of the church's Division of Racial Minorities), and M. Moran Weston (Rector of St. Philip's Church in Harlem, one of the largest parishes in the denomination). Writing in an editorial in *The Witness*, Stringfellow justly ridiculed the report in *The Episcopalian* for failing to acknowledge the degree to which racism infected the church. But rather than also applauding the fact that his black fellow church members had at last been accorded some recognition, he argued— from his perspective as a white theologian—that race should be regarded as totally irrelevant to the church's mission. To think that an article about a racial group was a sign of *progress*, then, simply proved how backward the church really was.[19]

As Stringfellow's reaction to the work of black Episcopalians suggests, the decade of the sixties was an extremely confusing time for those involved in the denomination's ministry among African Americans. On the one hand, white liberals (both inside and outside the Episcopal Church) assumed that "race" had become an outdated subject, and they sincerely believed that bigotry would disappear if categorization by race were eliminated altogether. Consequently, many church leaders pressed for the consolidation of black congregations into nearby white parishes. On the other hand, churches under the leadership of black clergy were among the few institutions African Americans operated on their own, relatively free from white control. Racially segregated parishes not only helped foster black independence, but also provided employment for African Americans. And when small black parishes were merged with larger white parishes in the sixties, black priests who had served as rectors and vicars in the segregated sphere usually found themselves without jobs, for they were seldom hired as clergy in the "integrated" churches. As a result, white Episcopalians like Stringfellow who pictured single-race parishes and schools as a scandal to the gospel unwittingly contributed to the continued marginalization of African Americans within their denomination.[20]

Although Stringfellow failed perhaps to consider how his opinions would be received by those in charge of black-led organizations, Moran Weston of St. Philip's, Harlem, called his attention to the problem. In a 1965 review essay, in which he discussed Stringfellow's autobiography, *My People Is the Enemy*, and other recent books on the civil rights movement, Weston dismissed Stringfellow as one of several "Caucasian authors" reaping undeserved benefits from the experiences of African Americans. While Stringfellow's observations had some merit, his language was often "coarse, inaccurate, and arrogant," and he was essentially "an 'enemy' of the people who treated him with courtesy and kindness" in Harlem. Stringfellow's worst fault was his insistence on downplaying the innate strength of African Americans in New York—those (like Weston himself) who had "survived with dignity, purpose, and achievement . . . in what others call the 'slums,' but what they call 'home.'" *My People Is the Enemy* might be acceptable as the reflections of a white man living in an environment that was alien to him, Weston surmised, but it was not a reliable description of real life on the streets of upper Manhattan.[21]

While Weston's conclusions were far too harsh and failed to credit the exceptional commitment that brought Stringfellow to Harlem in the first place, he was justifiably sensitive to a white person's inclination to judge the black community from a distorted perspective. In fact, ever since the debates over slavery in the mid-nineteenth century, white Americans of all ideological stripes had tended both to blur the distinctions between African Americans and to create archetypal images (such as "Sambo" and "Uncle Tom") that they freely projected upon the black community. Because African Americans seemed invisible to the average white person, stereotypes easily took hold even in the most progressive circles. Then in the sixties, thanks in part to the national media's newfound interest in black affairs, white liberals and radicals continued this destructive tradition by developing a new variation on an old racist theme. "True blacks," they decided, were not stable middle- or working-class African Americans but those people most alienated from mainstream society, i.e., street-corner hustlers, looters in ghetto riots, and—in the late sixties—the Black Panthers.[22]

White activists and denominational leaders in the Episcopal Church extended this already faulty analysis into the realm of ecclesiastical policy. Since African-American Episcopalians not only were thought to constitute the most privileged portion of the black community but also were generally dismissed as social climbers, most liberal white Episcopalians concluded that nonbelievers and secular groups, not their associates within the Episcopal Church, were the authentic representatives of black America to whom attention, moral support, and financial assistance were owed. As a result, by the late sixties black Episcopalians had been excluded from the decision-making processes in their church, even on matters relating to race. Eventually, in protest against this pattern of slighting their commitment to the church and out of chagrin that "inexperienced white Johnny-come-latelies" had supplanted them as authorities on African-American affairs, Weston and other black priests formed the Union of Black Clergy and Laity (now the Union of Black Episcopalians) at St. Philip's, Harlem, in early 1968. The founders of that organization resolved to identify and combat *all* forms of American racism, even that practiced by well-meaning white anti-racists in the Episcopal Church.[23]

Weston's critical evaluation of Stringfellow's writings, therefore, was part of a much broader controversy both within the Episcopal

Church and within American society as a whole. Understanding this background and the context in which Stringfellow worked adds special poignancy to his remarks (quoted at the beginning of this article) about the limitations of white liberalism. "Nice, white liberals in the North," he observed, might not hate African Americans in the obvious ways segregationists in the South did, yet they practiced a type of paternalism that could be just as damaging to interracial understanding as outright bigotry. While Stringfellow's theological views by no means fit the stereotype of a "nice, white liberal," and while his personal motives were certainly commendable, the social attitudes he reflected must still be criticized in the light of his own (quite correct) analysis of the American racial situation. Notwithstanding the whole-hearted support he and other white progressives gave to the civil rights movement, they sometimes failed to appreciate that it was not their prerogative to label a black leader an "Uncle Tom" or to decide who was worthy to be accorded recognition in the African-American community.[24]

Although American Christians have not yet realized the color-blind society and racially inclusive church William Stringfellow advocated, his words and actions continue to challenge the complacency of anyone today who believes that politics and spirituality are separable. Working as a lawyer in Harlem between 1956 and 1962, he engaged firsthand in service with the poorest members of society. He was a founding member of ESCRU and helped spread the gospel of Christian integrationism it espoused. He made headlines in 1963 and 1964 by speaking out against racism at the National Conference on Religion and Race and at the Episcopal General Convention. And, in the numerous books and articles he published throughout his career, he provided an insightful theological rationale for the participation of church members in social change. Indeed, during the heyday of the black freedom movement, no white Episcopalian voiced a greater concern for the plight of African Americans than did Stringfellow. Only one shortcoming marred his otherwise imposing record as an activist, and, though noteworthy, it was a fault shared by many in that era—a flaw engendered by too much, rather than too little, enthusiasm for the civil rights cause.

NOTES

1 William Stringfellow, "Through Dooms of Love," in *New Theology No. 2*, ed. Martin E. Marty and Dean G. Peerman (New York: Macmillan, 1965), 294-95.

2 Bruce Kenrick, *Come Out the Wilderness: The Story of East Harlem Protestant Parish* (New York: Harper and Row, 1962), 29-30, 65-69, 142-44; William Stringfellow, "Poverty, Piety, Charity and Mission," *Christian Century*, 78 (1961), 584; idem, *My People Is the Enemy: An Autobiographical Polemic* (New York: Holt, Rinehart and Winston, 1964), 3-4, 22-27, 85-86; Gibson Winter, "The Church in Suburban Captivity," *Christian Century*, 72 (1955): 1112-14; idem, *The Suburban Captivity of the Churches: An Analysis of Protestant Responsibility in the Expanding Metropolis* (Garden City, New York: Doubleday, 1961), passim; Paul Moore, Jr., *The Church Reclaims the City* (New York: Seabury Press, 1964), passim; Mel Schoonover, "A Personal Memoir," in Andrew W. McThenia, Jr., ed., *Radical Christian and Exemplary Lawyer: Honoring William Stringfellow* (Grand Rapids, Michigan: William B. Eerdmans Publishing, 1995), 49-50. For a discussion of projects similar to Stringfellow's work with the East Harlem Protestant Parish, see Ross W. Sanderson, *The Church Serves the Changing City* (New York: Harper and Row, 1955); C. Kilmer Myers, *Light the Dark Streets* (Greenwich, Connecticut: Seabury Press, 1957); Jenny Moore, *The People on Second Street* (New York: William Morrow, 1968).

3 Kenrick, *Come Out the Wilderness*, 46, 144; William Stringfellow, *A Second Birthday* (Garden City, New York: Doubleday, 1970), 36-37; idem, *My People Is the Enemy*, 93-96; "Episcopalians: Critic from Within," *Time* 83:23 (June 5, 1964), 72; Schoonover, "Personal Memoir," 49-50; Andrew W. McThenia, Jr., "Introduction: How This Celebration Began," in McThenia, ed., *Radical Christian and Exemplary Lawyer*, 14-15.

4 John B. Morris, memorandum to "Members of Committee on Program" [from Atlanta] (Nov. 2, 1959), Box 4, William Stringfellow Papers (Collection #4438), Rare and Manuscript Collections Division, Cornell University Library, Ithaca, New York; Arthur E.

Walmsley, memorandum to John Lassoe et al. from New York (Nov. 6, 1959), Box 4, Stringfellow Papers, Cornell University, Ithaca, New York; Aldon D. Morris, *The Origins of the Civil Rights Movement: Black Communities Organizing for Change* (New York: Free Press, 1984), 51-57; John L. Kater, Jr., "The Episcopal Society for Cultural and Racial Unity and Its Role in the Episcopal Church, 1959-1970," Ph.D. dissertation (McGill University, 1973), 31-34.

5 Claude Sitton, "Episcopal Group Held in Jackson," *New York Times* (Sept. 14, 1961), 32; "15 Episcopal Clerics Convicted in South," *New York Times* (Sept. 16, 1961), 1, 12; Kater, "The Episcopal Society for Cultural and Racial Unity and Its Role in the Episcopal Church," 34-39, 44-48.

6 William Stringfellow, letter to John Denham from New York (May 7, 1962), Box 6, William Stringfellow Papers (Collection #4438), Rare and Manuscript Collections Division, Cornell University Library, Ithaca, New York; idem, *A Private and Public Faith* (Grand Rapids, Michigan: William B. Eerdmans Publishing, 1962), 20-21; idem, "Race, the Church, and the Law," *The Episcopalian* 127:11 (November 1962), 31-34; idem, "The Freedom of God," *The Witness* 48:27 (Aug. 8, 1963), 10.

7 William Stringfellow, letter to Markus Barth from New York (May 8, 1962), Box 6, William Stringfellow Papers (Collection #4438), Rare and Manuscript Collections Division, Cornell University Library, Ithaca, New York; idem, letter to Ed [?] from New York (July 25, 1962), Box 6, Stringfellow Papers, Cornell University, Ithaca, New York; idem, "Karl Barth as Preacher in America," *The Witness* 47:24 (June 28, 1962), 12-13; idem, *A Private and Public Faith*, 7-8, 15-17, 20-21, 57, 74-75; idem, *Dissenter in a Great Society: A Christian View of America in Crisis* (New York: Holt, Rinehart and Winston, 1966), 130, 141, 158-61; idem, *A Second Birthday*, 150-52; idem, "A Theology for the World," *Christian Century* 79 (1962): 615-16; Eberhard Busch, *Karl Barth: His Life from Letters and Autobiographical Texts*, trans. John Bowden (Philadelphia: Fortress Press, 1976), 459-60.

8 Mathew Ahmann, letter to William Stringfellow from Chicago (Feb.

28, 1963), Box 7, William Stringfellow Papers (Collection #4438), Rare and Manuscript Collections Division, Cornell University Library, Ithaca, New York; *Episcopal Society for Cultural and Racial Unity: Newsletter* (March 10, 1963), 5; Mathew Ahmann, ed., *Race: Challenge to Religion* (Chicago: Regnery, 1963), v-x, 1-6, 171-173; James F. Findlay, Jr., *Church People in the Struggle: The National Council of Churches and the Black Freedom Movement, 1950-1970* (New York: Oxford University Press, 1993), 32-33.

9 John B. Morris, letter to William Stringfellow from Atlanta (Jan. 28, 1963), Box 7, William Stringfellow Papers (Collection #4438), Rare and Manuscript Collections Division, Cornell University Library, Ithaca, New York; Sarah Patton Boyle, letter to [William] Stringfellow from Charlottesville, Virginia (Jan. 15, 1963), Box 7, Stringfellow Papers, Cornell University, Ithaca, New York; William Stringfellow, "Care Enough To Weep" (transcript, Jan. 14-17, 1963), Box 7, Stringfellow Papers, Cornell University, Ithaca, New York; idem, "Care Enough To Weep," *The Witness* 48:7 (Feb. 21, 1963), 13-15; idem, "Corny If Not Profane," *Christian Century* 80 (1963): 1135-36; Barbara G. Kremer, "For All of God's Children," *The Episcopalian* 128:3 (March 1963), 36-39; Will D. Campbell, *Brother to a Dragonfly* (New York: Seabury Press, 1977), 229-231. For appreciative comments on Stringfellow's remarks by African-American participants at the conference, see Benjamin E. Mays, *Born to Rebel: An Autobiography* (New York: Scribner's, 1971), 262-263; Anna Arnold Hedgeman, *The Gift of Chaos: Decades of American Discontent* (New York: Oxford University Press, 1977), 50-51.

10 "Race Relations: Birmingham and After," *The Episcopalian* 128:7 (July 1963), 33-35; Thomas LaBar, "A Summer of Significance," *The Episcopalian,* 128:9 (September 1963), 19-21; Robert Weisbrot, *Freedom Bound: A History of America's Civil Rights Movement* (New York: Penguin, 1990), 68-70; Findlay, *Church People in the Struggle*, 33-34.

11 Stringfellow, "Episcopalians: Critic from Within," 72; idem, "Race, Religion and Revenge," *Christian Century* 79 (1962): 192-194; idem, *My People Is the Enemy*, 105-112, 133-141; McThenia,

"Introduction," 15; Paul D. West, "Bibliography: The Works of William Stringfellow," in *A Keeper of the Word: Selected Writings of William Stringfellow*, ed. Bill Wylie-Kellermann (Grand Rapids, Michigan: William B. Eerdmans Publishing, 1994), 417-19.

12 William Stringfellow, letter to Bill Spofford from Aarhus, Denmark (Aug. 13, 1964), Box 8, William Stringfellow Papers (Collection #4438), Rare and Manuscript Collections Division, Cornell University Library, Ithaca, New York; John B. Morris, letter to William Stringfellow from Atlanta (Sept. 30, 1964), Box 59, Episcopal Society for Cultural and Racial Unity Records, King Library and Archives, Martin Luther King, Jr., Center, Atlanta; William Stringfellow, "A Statement of Conscience on Racism in the Presidential Campaign" (Oct. 13, 1964), Box 8, Stringfellow Papers, Cornell University, Ithaca, New York; Press Release (Oct. 19, 1964), Box 8, Stringfellow Papers, Cornell University, Ithaca, New York; William Stringfellow, "God, Guilt and Goldwater," *Christian Century* 81 (1964): 1079-83; "Bill Stringfellow Also Signs," *The Witness* 49:27 (Aug. 6, 1964), 6; "Christian Conscience and the Election," *The Witness* 49:27 (Aug. 6, 1964), 7; Kater, "The Episcopal Society for Cultural and Racial Unity and Its Role in the Episcopal Church," 67-69; Weisbrot, *Freedom Bound*, 123-126.

13 John B. Morris, letter to "Dear Friend" from Atlanta (Nov. 12, 1964), Box 8, William Stringfellow Papers (Collection #4438), Rare and Manuscript Collections Division, Cornell University Library, Ithaca, New York; idem, letter to Bill [Stringfellow] from Atlanta (Nov. 12, 1964) Box 9, Stringfellow Papers, Cornell University, Ithaca, New York; William Stringfellow, letter to Vera Bollton from New York (Nov. 23, 1964), Box 8, Stringfellow Papers, Cornell University, Ithaca, New York; [idem], letter to John Morris from New York (Nov. 25, 1964), Box 9, Stringfellow Papers, Cornell University, Ithaca, New York; *Journal of the General Convention of the Protestant Episcopal Church* (1964), 144, 167, 372-73; "To Rectify a Charge," *The Living Church* 149:19 (Nov. 8, 1964), 9; Thomas LaBar, "General Convention 1964," *The Episcopalian* 129:12 (December 1964), 4, 8; Kater, "The Episcopal Society for Cultural and Racial Unity and Its Role in the Episcopal Church," 69-70.

14 Martin Luther King, Jr., "I Have a Dream," in *A Testament of Hope: The Essential Writings of Martin Luther King, Jr.*, ed. James Melvin Washington (San Francisco: Harper and Row, 1986), 217; Robert S. Ellwood, *The Sixties Spiritual Awakening: American Religion Moving from Modern to Postmodern* (New Brunswick, New Jersey: Rutgers University Press, 1994), 120-121; David Steigerwald, *The Sixties and the End of Modern America* (New York: St. Martin's Press, 1995), 201-2; Weisbrot, *Freedom Bound*, 88-92, 154-64; Findlay, *Church People in the Struggle*, 64-65.

15 Jonathan Daniels, handwritten note to William Stringfellow at the end of a letter to C.C.J. Carpenter from Selma, Alabama (April 21, 1965), Box 10, William Stringfellow Papers (Collection #4438), Rare and Manuscript Collections Division, Cornell University Library, Ithaca, New York; [William Stringfellow], letter to Jonathan Daniels from New York (May 18, 1965), Box 10, Stringfellow Papers, Cornell University, Ithaca, New York; idem, "A Plenary Requiem" [1965], Box 9, Stringfellow Papers, Cornell University, Ithaca, New York; idem, "A Few Words on Behalf of a Friend Recently Dead," *Episcopal Society for Cultural and Racial Unity Newsletter* (Oct. 28, 1965), addendum; idem, "Moved Not by Wrath but Despair," *Churchman* 179:7 (July, 1965), 10-11; "Stringfellow Claims Churchmen Apathetic to Rights Drive," *The Witness* 50:27 (Aug. 19, 1965), 6. Jonathan Daniels taught remedial reading to black children in the summer of 1965. He died from a gunshot wound sustained on Aug. 20, 1965. His life is commemorated in the Episcopal Calendar of the Church Year on August 14.

16 William Stringfellow, "Poverty and Christian Response," *The Witness* 50:1 (Jan. 7, 1965), 8-10; idem, "Sin, Morality and Poverty," *Christian Century* 82 (1965): 703-706; idem, "The Great Society as a Myth," *The Witness* 51:37 (Nov. 17, 1966), 9, 14; idem, *Dissenter in a Great Society*, 140-143; idem, *My People Is the Enemy*, 85-96; "Selma, Civil Rights, and the Church Militant," *Newsweek* 65:13 (March 29, 1965), 78.

17 William Stringfellow, "Harlem, Rebellion and Resurrection," *Christian Century* 87 (Nov. 11, 1970): 1345-48; idem and Anthony

Towne, *The Bishop Pike Affair: Scandals of Conscience and Heresy, Relevance and Solemnity in the Contemporary Church* (New York: Harper and Row, 1967), 196-197; Stringfellow, *A Simplicity of Faith: My Experience in Mourning* (Nashville: Abingdon Press, 1982), 87; idem, *A Second Birthday*, 17-20, 37, 130; Kwame Ture [Stokely Carmichael] and Charles V. Hamilton, *Black Power: The Politics of Liberation in America* (1967; New York: Vintage Books, 1992), 44-47; Steigerwald, *The Sixties and the End of Modern America*, 60-62; Weisbrot, *Freedom Bound*, 196-204, 246-47. For Stringfellow's comments on the Black Manifesto's demand that churches and synagogues pay $500 million in reparations for the historic evils white Americans had committed against African Americans, see press release, "Opponents of Reparations Warned to Abstain from Lord's Supper" (October 12, [1969]), Box 14, William Stringfellow Papers (Collection #4438), Rare and Manuscript Collections Division, Cornell University Library, Ithaca, New York; William Stringfellow, "A Postscript to South Bend: Dare White Episcopalians Receive Holy Communion Anymore?" [October 1969], Box 14, Stringfellow Papers, Cornell University, Ithaca, New York; William Stringfellow, "Reparations: Repentance as a Necessity to Reconciliation," in *Black Manifesto: Religion, Racism, and Reparations*, eds. Robert S. Lecky and H. Elliott Wright (New York: Sheed and Ward, 1969), 52-64.

18 Gunnar Myrdal, *An American Dilemma: The Negro Problem and Modern Democracy* (New York: Harper and Row, 1962), 858-63, 873-78, 928-29, 936-41, 952-53; Stringfellow, "Race, Religion and Revenge," 192-94; idem, *A Private and Public Faith*, 21-22; idem, *My People Is the Enemy*, 78-80, 84, 114, 118-120, 137-138; David W. Southern, *Gunnar Myrdal and Black-White Relations: The Use and Abuse of* An American Dilemma, *1944-1969* (Baton Rouge: Louisiana State University Press, 1987), 66-68, 94-95. For a more appreciative discussion of the social contributions of African-American Christianity, see C. Eric Lincoln, *The Black Church Since Frazier* (New York: Schocken Books, 1974), 107-10; Peter J. Paris, *The Social Teaching of the Black Churches* (Philadelphia: Fortress Press, 1985), 1-10, 86-88, 133-34; C. Eric Lincoln and Lawrence H. Mamiya, *The Black Church and the African American Experience*

(Durham, North Carolina: Duke University Press, 1990), 11-16, 197-204.

19 "The Negro Episcopalian," *The Episcopalian* 127:3 (March, 1962), 19-42; William Stringfellow, "The White Episcopalian," [April 1962], Box 6, William Stringfellow Papers (Collection #4438), Rare and Manuscript Collections Division, Cornell University Library, Ithaca, New York; "Let's Have a White Episcopalian Issue," *The Witness* 47:16 (April 26, 1962), 7; Morris, *The Origins of the Civil Rights Movement*, 40-76. Since Stringfellow's editorial also criticized ESCRU for implicitly setting itself apart from the rest of the church in its approach to race relations, his remarks received a sharp rejoinder in the next newsletter of that organization—see [John B. Morris], "The Witness—On and Off," *Episcopal Society for Cultural and Racial Unity Newsletter* (June 10, 1962), 10.

20 Harold T. Lewis, *Yet With a Steady Beat: The African American Struggle for Recognition in the Episcopal Church* (Valley Forge, Pennsylvania: Trinity Press International, 1996), 139, 152-55; Southern, *Gunnar Myrdal and Black-White Relations*, 199-200; Morris, *Origins of the Civil Rights Movement*, 4-12.

21 M. Moran Weston, "The Crisis—in Black and White," *The Living Church* 150:21 (May 23, 1965), 14-16; "Harlem's Banker-Priest," *Ebony* 24:5 (March, 1969), 92-94, 98, 100.

22 Joel Williamson, *A Rage for Order: Black/White Relations in the American South Since Emancipation* (New York: Oxford University Press, 1986), 233-37, 250-51; Hugh Pearson, *The Shadow of the Panther: Huey Newton and the Price of Black Power in America* (Reading, Massachusetts: Addison-Wesley, 1994), 338-40.

23 John M. Burgess, letter to Daniel Corrigan from Boston (Jan. 8, 1968), in folder 113-2-11, Records of the Presiding Bishop of the Episcopal Church, Archives of the Episcopal Church, Austin, Texas; idem, *Black Gospel/White Church* (New York: Seabury Press, 1982), 45; "Wright Wrangle," *The Living Church* 155:15 (Oct. 8, 1967), 14; Willard B. Gatewood, *Aristocrats of Color: The Black Elite, 1880-1920* (Bloomington, Indiana: Indiana University Press, 1990), 272-77; Edward Rodman, *Let There Be Peace Among Us: A Story of the*

Union of Black Episcopalians (Lawrenceville, Virginia: Brunswick, 1990), 3-7; Lewis, *Yet With a Steady Beat*, 1-4, 58-60, 155-59.

24 Stringfellow, "Through Dooms of Love," 293-95; idem, *Dissenter in a Great Society*, 120-22.

STRINGFELLOW
AND THE LAW

JOHN M. GESSELL

In any polity, republic, or society, law and theology are constitutive
of order and meaning. Without order and meaning there can be no
polity, only a jumble of persons. Law is the formal description of the
polity and the sinews of its order and organization. Theology is the
discriminate critique of the polity and its laws, and the articulation of
its meaning and purpose. When the laws are subverted and theology
is scorned, the polity sinks into chaos and inanity and ceases to be
seminal. It can no longer support and nourish the human spirit and
human enterprises.

In ancient times the mark of the crucial importance of law was
the theory that it was a gift of the gods or that it was ascribed to the
marvelous achievement of an inspired and wise lawgiver. Such men
were remembered forever in the history of the polity like Solomon
and Moses. Law was the gift of genius and human life depended on
this. The well-ordering of the polity was a prize to be grasped and a
protection against the ever-threatening forces of chaos, disorder, and
meaninglessness. In classical polities the punishment for disruption
of the order of the polity by insurrection or by some act of pollution
was often death.

Law is not autonomous. It is neither its own judge, nor its own
end. It does not constitute its own purpose. Law is a function of the

polity and is the formal constitution of the polity. But it is always ideally under the judgment of theology and accountable to it. This is to say that law is subject to critical revision and to the judgment of a theonomous principle beyond itself.

In the examination of Bill Stringfellow's thought on faith, church, and politics in a post-modern world, we must start with the relation of law and faith, because Stringfellow was a lawyer and a Christian, and because that is where he started. He always sought to make clear that law, while of critical importance, was always to be understood under the aspect of the principle of theonomy. He wrote in 1958 in *The Church Review* that the relation between Christianity and the legal profession is first of all conversion which exposes both alienation from work and the world, and also the reality of faithlessness "moving toward a restoration in faith of a sacramental significance of work."[1]

In any polity, offenses may come, but it is not the law that is the offender. The offense, rather, is those who bend the law toward injustice for their own self-aggrandizing purposes. While the law has built-in safeguards against its misuse, these safeguards must be employed in light of an external critical theonomous principle. Unless these critical principles are enforced, the law becomes a party to the debauching and destruction of the polity. It is this that Bill Stringfellow contested all of his life from the time of his Harlem law practice among the poor, to his defense of Bishop Pike and Father Wendt, to his reproaches against Bishop Allin, to his defense of Daniel Berrigan. Stringfellow's legal vocation as theologian and lawyer was to defend the law and to call into sharp question those who would use it for their own purposes to the destruction of the polity.

Stringfellow saw the challenge of the law as an instrument for sorting out the problems of human nature—cupidity and justice, good and evil, fairness and exploitation, poverty and affluence. Somewhere he wrote that law justly administered is a response to the Word of God.[2] This is the law under the aspect of the theonomous principle, doing what it was meant to do as constitutive of the polity. The law is capable of expressing a form of truth, balancing competing interests. Without this there can be no achievement of a relatively just society.

Stringfellow, then, held a functional view of the law. He states in a *Vanderbilt Law Review* article,

The tension between law and grace is such that there is no Christian jurisprudence. There is not a particular philosophy of law which has special integrity in the Gospel. Nor is there a way really to make the positive law or the ethics of law, the purposes of law which men offer as a measure for positive legislation, compatible with the Gospel.

This does not at all mean that Christians disregard the law, rather they regard it for exactly and only what it is: law and justice are the manner in which men maintain themselves in history. Law is a condition of historical existence, a circumstance of the fall. Christians, both in the congregation and in dispersion, are in the world, living in history, under the sanctions of secular law, and this is the locus of their proclamation of the Gospel for the world. For law, the proclamation of the Gospel means, in the first instance, the comprehension that law, though sometimes it can name sin, originates itself in sin and cannot overcome the power of sin."[3]

Law is descriptive of community or polity. It defines the membership of those who are willing to subscribe to the law. It defines boundaries, including all of those within the polity who accept the law as their law by which they are willing to live their lives in the polity, and excludes scofflaws as outlaws, those who run outside the polity and who defy its laws.

A functional view of the law holds law, not as an instrument for its own autonomous ends or one of those principalities which must secure its own triumph, but as instrumental to securing the common good. The law, in this view, is organic and arises out of the common life of the polity and is accepted consensually by members of the polity. This view is akin to some of the classical contractualist theories of polity from Jean Bodin and Althusius to Hobbes, Locke, and Rousseau. This embraces enlightenment theories of freedom and human rights. I am aware of contemporary critiques of enlightenment theories of freedom but would argue that the apparent failure of the law in this regard is not so much that the theory is wrong, but that insufficient energy has been directed toward the vigilance required to make it work in practice.

Law describes a community in which all share a common bond and a common purpose which make possible a high level of individual effort and achievement in the context of an ordered polity.[4] Law, therefore, describes the community from which it derives, orders its common life, locates its boundaries, and internally prescribes the principles and procedures of the primacy of due process, equity, and the rule of law.

Stringfellow's view of the law is concretely realized in two types of struggle in which he was involved off and on for most of his life. These struggles are epitomized in his experience of the failure of advocacy in Harlem, and the failure of due process in church affairs. I shall examine these in turn below.

The critical importance of attending to Stringfellow's life-long critique is clear in current events. The law, as noted above, cannot be autonomous. It has no built-in principle of self-criticism and correction. It can be unscrupulously corrupted and subverted to the ends of special interests, and used as an oppressive instrument (under the guise, ironically, of legality) of the powerful against the powerless, contrary to the intentions of the lawgivers.

Several instances come to mind. The U.S. Environmental Protection Agency, more often than not, resists enforcing the regulations it was established to oversee, and opposes congressional attempts to pass stricter environmental laws. In protecting the interests of polluters it forsakes the public interest. Further, the misuse of law and the probable failure of due process in the trial of Manuel Noriega may open the way for pragmatic and selective use of the law and to establish that foreign defendants outside the U.S. are not covered by the fundamental protections of the Constitution. As Justice Brennan observed, "If we seek respect for law and order, we must observe these principles ourselves." Another instance is the troublesome development, since the Reagan years, of the use of Rule 11 (a federal procedure originally created to punish lawyers and plaintiffs who file suits that will not stand up to factual scrutiny) to strike down cases such as civil-rights, human rights and public-interest suits by conservative judges who find these suits and their lawyers personally offensive.

Stringfellow was extraordinarily sensitive to the misuse and the failure of the law to protect the powerful and to oppress the weak. In his writings, either addressing the law directly in law school journals, or in his general writings in which the discussion of the law arises in context, he addressed this issue by appealing to theological and ethical principles as a theonomous critique of legal subterfuge and distortion. For the law to function properly, and as it should in the polity, it must be subject to the discriminate principle of theonomy. An example of this comprehensive critical acumen concerning the law and Christian faith is found in *Federation News*. He states, "In the exploration of the relation of theology and law as a movement beyond mere legal pragmatism, there is danger that a natural law jurisprudence will be all that is recovered. This would be unfaithful to the gospel."[5]

Stringfellow engages the theonomous critique of law by appealing to fundamental principles of justice and equity as set forth in the western moral tradition and in Christian theology, and by the presence of the Christian lawyer who can be expected to make such appeals when appropriate. He himself over his lifetime was the model of the theonomous witnessing presence. He invoked the ideal Christian lawyer as the bearer of this critique, which is a vocational act. An examination of his periodical writing on the law, lawyers, and the Christian faith exhibits this point as do his autobiographical writings such as *My People Is the Enemy*. His critique even reached the conventional interpretation of the constitution itself which implicitly contributes to the malaise of American life and its voluntarism and rootless individualism. Stringfellow views the "separation" clause of Article 1 of the Bill of Rights as not only self-contradictory, but pernicious. It does not in fact successfully separate religion and politics, church and state. The law supports and encourages, shows a preference for, a particular theology and a specific polity. It is a polity of disunity based on radical individualism embodied in the law. This is inconsistent with the professed neutrality between religious denominations.[6]

One of the results of this is the distortion of the function of the law itself and what Stringfellow calls the crisis in confidence in the legal profession. He writes of "an increasingly political use, or abuse, of the law . . . under authority that . . . proceeds to rule as a law unto itself, without the discipline of due process or similar restraints . . . ." Thus, he writes, "the rampant operative jurisprudence in this society would be called positivism," and legal ethics is generally "so narrow a form of ethics as to be impotent."[7]

Stringfellow's actual physical presence in the streets of Harlem in the fifties and sixties gives immediacy and poignancy to his witness to the oppression he found there. "I came to Harlem to live, to work there as a lawyer, to take some part in the politics of the neighborhood, to be a layman in the Church there . . . . I am only a witness, testifying as accurately as I am able, to what I myself have seen and heard during the time I lived and worked in Harlem."[8]

Stringfellow reports that he perceived in the internal life in the ghetto the political structures, upheld by a legality, which enforced poverty and racism at a terrible cost to the poor and the oppressed.[9] Some black members of the community benefited from this corruption, but most paid the cost.

The cost, he saw, went beyond Harlem. He states, ". . . the health and maturity of the *American legal system* [italics added] depend upon whether or not those who are the outcasts in society—the poor, the socially discriminated against, the politically unpopular—are, as a practical matter, represented in their rights and complaints and causes before the law."[10]

And a further corruption of the law is a consequence. In the *North Dakota Law Review* William Stringfellow wrote,

> . . . poverty in America means the hostility of the law and of the administration of the law to the interests and rights, causes and complaints of those who are poor . . . . For the poor, especially for the poor confined to the Negro ghettos in the cities, the impression that the law is hostile to them is implanted in a multitude of ways . . . . [T]he only image of the law which is credible, from the point of view of the outcast, is of the law as a symbol of their rejection by society . . . . [The law serves] property rights to the neglect of human rights . . . . [The law thus] jeopardizes the whole of society, not just the poor.[11]

He also found out that

> politics has not provided fundamental remedy for the poverty of East Harlem . . . where political power represents economic investment, whether lawful or criminal, [and] the poor are apt to be excluded from politics . . . . But if a lawyer . . . [is to] be

immersed in the life of the place where he practices, then the law itself must be genuinely implicated in and wrought from the realities of human existence. This would help free the law from pretentious moralism and from superstition and obsolescence as well .... [But] the law is not only obsolete in this instance and indifferent to crucial facts about the matter with which it deals, but I would argue that it works vindictively .... In short, the issue for the law is whether it stands at the intersection of life, aware of the self-interest of adverse contentions, free to be the advocate of each.[12]

This pessimistic assessment was never to be substantially revised. Five years later he wrote autobiographically in *My People Is the Enemy:*

To be concerned with the outcast is an echo, of course, of the Gospel itself. Characteristically, the Christian is to be found in his work and witness in the world among those for whom no one else cares—the poor, the sick, the imprisoned, the misfits, the homeless, the orphans and beggars. The presence of the Christian among the outcasts is the way in which the Christian represents, concretely, the ubiquity and universality of the intercession of Christ for all men. All men are encompassed in the ministry of the Christian to the least of men. I had to find out more about the meaning of that, too.

What I found out—what I found out theologically—from my stay in Harlem is, of course, that all men are outcasts in one sense or another. It is only more vivid that men are outcasts in a place like Harlem. No man, however, escapes this condition; no man avoids alienation from other men; no man evades the Fall.

Unhappily, what I found out is that, for the most part, the outcasts of this society—those who live somehow on its fringes, are not usually or effectively or even honestly represented before the law. Most are simply not represented at all. They can't afford the law, or they are so uninformed as to their rights that they do not pursue them, or they are so disenchanted by what they know or hear of the administration of the law that they have no confidence that their rights will be vindicated.[13]

Nor was Stringfellow to discover grounds for reassurance as he later became involved in church advocacy related to the cases of Bishop Pike and Father Wendt. In what he called the *Bishop Pike Affair,* he sets the terms for concern.

The Bishop Pike Affair has a symbolic importance for many persons outside the precincts of contemporary Christendom as well as for multitudes within the Episcopal Church or other churches.

One aspect of the interest of such outsiders is manifestly religious and theological, though not sectarian or dogmatic. The involvement of some who reject—or are rejected by—the traditional churches in protest movements, in experimentation with psychedelic drugs, in "be-ins," represents a quest for meaning and, sometimes, an affirmation of life which is essential and even profoundly religious. It can be cogently argued that, in comparison to the "hippies," creedal literalists in the churches are a variety of nihilists. No doubt the latter find the former vulgar, just as they do Bishop Pike, but the controversy surrounding Bishop Pike evokes the sympathy and respect of those outside the churches because they can at least recognize in the bishop a Christian, and an ecclesiastic at that, who is living in the present century.

There is another dimension to the public concern with the Bishop Pike affair, however, which, in lawyer's language, is designated by the term "due process of law." In one case in Alabama, which the authorities and citizens of that jurisdiction have not always borne in mind, due process of law is thus defined:

Due process of law implies the right of the person affected thereby to be present before the tribunal which pronounces judgment upon the question of life, liberty or property . . . to be heard . . . and to have the right of controverting, by proof, every material fact. (Quoted from Zeigler vs. Railroad Co., 58 Ala. 599)

Put differently and more directly, with respect to Bishop Pike, due process raises the question of whether or not Bishop Pike had a fair hearing at Wheeling, or in the events prior to the censure, or in the subsequent happenings, *and* whether he can or will ever obtain such, considering what has so far occurred, given the inherited procedures for heresy trials in the Episcopal Church, and taking the relevant ecclesiastical and civil precedents into account.[14]

Stringfellow concurs, as he says, with many observers at the time of the Pike censure that Pike was not treated fairly. Due process he argues is the crux, the central issue here. But the Pike affair demonstrates with what difficulty it was to come by truth and fairness in the church, and "demonstrates the low estate of due process in ecclesiastical institutions . . . . The poor esteem for due process seems particularly poignant in the

Episcopal Church because of its historic origins in the Church of England and, thus, special connections with Anglo-Saxon common law."[15]

Stringfellow painstakingly, meticulously, in detail, analyzes with care the intricacies of the Pike affair in order to lay out the errors, procedural defects, lack of specificity, and clarity in the charges and proposed presentments, the conflicts of interest, the denial to the accused the right to face his accusers and to defend himself. All of these matters raise doubts that due process was or could have been observed. This, together with, above all, an expediency in the proceedings simply meant, Stringfellow avers, that justice could not be rendered and that in some sense the affair has never been resolved. Stringfellow called the censure procedure used by the House of Bishops of the Episcopal Church against Bishop Pike in connection with alleged charges of heresy scandalous and seriously defective as to the use of due process. The censure was, he said, an "inherent profanity." The failure of due process in the case involved, he noted, "risks to liberty, property, humiliation and bodily harm."[16]

The Bishop Pike affair had to do with the attempt to clarify and modernize opaque theological language and hence the doctrinal clarity of the truth of the church's claims. This was a keen interest of Stringfellow, and he contributed to this search for clarity as an enhancement of the church's mission to the world. Unhappily, the Pike affair did not make its maximum contribution to this urgent concern. Stringfellow joined in the Wendt cause which arose in connection with the controversy surrounding the ordination of women in the Episcopal Church. While this also was an attempt to secure greater clarity in the church's theology, it was as well an attempt to achieve canonical clarity. As Stringfellow made clear, there was also here much canonical confusion.

In this connection Stringfellow wrote,

> The controversy has reached a juncture that preaches degeneracy. The Episcopal Church is in a state of dysfunction, or, if it can be said to be working as an institution, it is so only in a grossly inappropriate manner. Recall what has happened:
>
> At the so-called emergency meeting of the House of Bishops at O'Hare Airport last August, the presiding bishop stated, and it

was then widely disseminated by the official, national press agency of the church, that the bishops had "ruled" the Philadelphia ordination "invalid" despite the truth that the House of Bishops lacks juridical or legislative competence to utter any such ruling.

That misrepresentation—and defamation—left the new priests little alternative except to affirm their ordinations straightforwardly by exercising their priesthood respectively where invited by parishes or missions to do so.

No canonical charges have been prosecuted against any of the Philadelphia priests and, in fact, there has been an elaborate strategy to avoid ecclesiastical trials of those women.

Similarly, the Board of Inquiry convened to investigate charges against the ordaining bishops resorted to fantastic and convoluted exegesis of the heresy canon in order to evade their trials.

Meanwhile, two rectors—William Wendt and Peter Beebe—who, with the support of their vestries and parishioners, invited women priests to preside at celebrations of the Eucharist have been tried and convicted in diocesan courts.

None of these events need have happened. There is no canonical impediment to the ordination of women in the Episcopal Church. The various dioceses are free and able to ordain women as priests now. It is custom only that is challenged; the canon law or the church constitution requires no alteration, addition, or amendment. The General Convention may legislate, but such is not a mandatory prerequisite for the ordination of women by dioceses disposed to ordain women to the priesthood.[17]

But the trial and conviction of Father Wendt revealed another, probably more serious matter, the ignorance, contempt, and neglect of the Church's polity and canons at the highest levels. In connection with defending Wendt in the ecclesiastical court in the Diocese of Washington, Stringfellow subpoenaed the Presiding Bishop of the Episcopal Church, John Allin. Bishop Allin ignored the subpoena. Later, Stringfellow took Allin sharply to task for this and other negligences in his now famous letter, which is here excerpted.

For these years of your incumbency as presiding bishop, I have hoped, as have so many others, that you would sometime evince a strong and definite conviction concerning the mission of the church in this world and, particularly, that of the Episcopal Church in contemporary U.S. society. None has been forthcoming. Instead, you have again and again manifested an absence of conviction, a failure of candor, a spirit of confusion, a double-mindedness, a tendency to tailor utterance to the circumstances of the moment. Your image of ambivalence and elusiveness was noticeable throughout the controversy attending the ordination of women, after your initial hysteria about the Philadelphia ordinations subsided. It was not until after the general convention had acted definitively that you confided your skepticism about the vocation of women as priests, and then you did so in a manner that seemed calculated to incite defiance or circumvention of the law of the church. In consequence, the so-called conscience clause has been inflated far beyond the scope of conscientious dissent or protest into a virtual act of nullification that jeopardizes the efficacy of canon law and scandalizes the very polity of the Episcopal Church.

All of this had been foreshadowed, of course, in the Wendt trial in the ecclesiastical court in the diocese of Washington, when in violation of your canonical duty you defied the subpoena of the court to appear and testify, and were thereupon duly adjudged in contempt of that court. You have done nothing to purge yourself of that contempt.[18]

But even more serious in Stringfellow's view was the FBI raid on the Episcopal Church headquarters in New York City on November 18, 1976. In an editorial which I wrote for the *St. Luke's Journal of Theology* I attempted to indicate the critical issues. I spoke of the threat to civil and religious liberties which I believe the case posed by the recent handling of

. . . the FBI's visit to the Episcopal Church Center, and the response to a federal Grand Jury in New York City and its subpoenaing of a staff member, Ms. Maria Cueto, and her secretary, Raisa Nemikin.

Briefly, the FBI and a Grand Jury have been searching since last fall for links alleged to exist between the Episcopal Church's National Commission on Hispanic Affairs (NCHA) and a Puerto Rican independence movement (FALN), a self-styled terrorist group which has claimed responsibility for some bombings in New York and Chicago.

Ms. Cueto and Ms. Nemikin answered all of the questions put to them by the FBI and identified Carlos Albert Torres of FALN as a member of the Commission. They refused to testify before the Grand Jury, however, on grounds that it was conducting "a fishing expedition to intimidate, harass, frighten and prevent the church. . . from effectively carrying out its [sic] Christian mission and ministry to oppressed and forgotten minorities in the U.S.," and that by responding they would violate the confidence and trust of persons working with the Hispanic Commission.

In connection with this case, last November FBI agents made a sweep of the offices at the Episcopal Church Center without careful specification as to what was being sought and without adequate supervision.

At this point Ms. Cueto and Ms. Nemikin remain jailed for the duration of the term of the New York Grand Jury.

Aside from the inept and insensitive handling of this matter the complex series of events surrounding it raise several significant questions relative to issues of the gospel and justice. One set of questions has to do with the credibility of the mission of the church, and another with the church's complicity with the state.

In connection with the first, throwing into question the credibility of the mission of the church, the action of the Episcopal Church in this instance has had the effect of jeopardizing all churches in their work for justice and cooperation with the oppressed, and especially with Hispanic minorities in this country. As Arthur Lloyd has written in *Plumbline* (April 1977), by failing to express effective solidarity with the two women in their witness, a theology of church has been enacted, the church as the servant of the state. All of this compromises the credibility of the church, its mission, and its freedom to proclaim the gospel.

With regard to the second, church-state relations, there is sufficient data to support the conclusions of several observers that, in this case at least, civil authority has attempted to define and limit the mission of the church by defining the scope of the church's ministry and the role of church staff persons in that ministry. The extreme of this development is a church co-opted by the state and, as the two women have stated, setting a precedent that will permit the church to cooperate inadvertently in repressive measures through which the government will attempt to isolate and make the church's work ineffective. The "chilling effect" of the decision to make available to the FBI the NCHA records since 1970 can scarcely be underestimated.

> Another aspect of this case is the church's complicity with the
> state in illegal acts related to Grand Jury and FBI abuses. This pos-
> sibility does not appear to be recognized by any of the statements
> issued from the Episcopal Church Center. It must be pointed out
> that there are ample precedent and documentation for the morali-
> ty of refusing to testify before a Grand Jury under "use immuni-
> ty." The church can be judged for its failure to raise critical ques-
> tions concerning the uses of state power in this instance.[19]

Many questions arising out of this notorious case remain unan-
swered to this day. These questions touch on matters of justice and
the failure of due process. Widespread notice was taken in the church
press. Comment was contained in two consecutive issues of *The
Witness*, March and April 1977. And in its issue of May 2, 1977,
Christianity and Crisis contained an article by Dean Kelley calling
the Episcopal Church leadership sharply to task for its part in the
affair.[20] Stringfellow was then a contributing editor of *Christianity
and Crisis*.

By this time, it seems to me, Stringfellow had begun to despair
of the ability of the law to guard due process and to deliver justice
either in church or civil state. He was a keen interpreter of biblical
texts who, at about this time, gave sustained attention in two books
to the biblical insights into those demonic forces and powers which
are capable of creating chaos and disruption. The demonic, he said,
becomes institutionalized in the principalities of church and state.[21]
The arrest of Daniel Berrigan and the indictments of William
Stringfellow and Anthony Towne for allegedly "concealing"
Berrigan at their Block Island home disclosed the demonic oppression and tyrannical power of the state.[22] He began, as he says, slowly to see the "law as an aggressor."[23] This is the measure of how his
mind had changed.

The FBI raid and subsequent events disclosed to Stringfellow
(and to anyone willing to look in that direction) the demonizing of
the church. A further excerpt from the "Open Letter" makes clear
Stringfellow's theological perspective. To Bishop Allin he writes

> There are those who refer to you as a "conservative," but that is
> hyperbole. Such disrespect for the law of the church as you have
> shown and encouraged is not a conservative trait.

I attribute this behavior, rather, to a lack of conviction, or to expediency, which, lamentable in any circumstances, is essentially incongruous to the office you hold. That is why I have mentioned, now and then, that I would much prefer as presiding bishop a vigorous and principled reactionary. At least, then, there could be disagreement and dispute in the church that would be candid and wholesome. As it is, instead of leadership, in these past six years, there has been aimlessness.

Yet aimless is not the same as harmless. You have not been in a situation of the bland leading the bland if only because so many have suffered so much harm on your account, whether by reason of deliberate intent or omission. After all, it cannot be overlooked that your improvidence occasioned the imprisonment of two church employees, facilitated the subsequent imprisonment of even other Hispanics, and seriously impaired the constitutionally sanctioned freedom of the churches in this country. Nor can the countless hassles, obstinacies, and discriminations encountered by women qualified and called to ordination as priests be overlooked. Nor can the cruel and hypocritical attitude toward the ordination of homosexuals. Nor can the neglect of all the other issues between the church and this society whilst the dissipation of sham debates and churchy charades continues.

Leadership could have made a difference in all of these matters, but, alas, the Episcopal Church has been deprived of leadership. When you were elected at the Louisville general convention a void opened in the leadership of the Episcopal Church, which has been filled by management. In the church, as with other principalities and powers, management is preoccupied with institutional preservation and with condiments of statistical prosperity. To management, substantive controversy is perceived as threatening per se, rather than as a sign of vitality, and conformity to the mere survival interest of the institution gains domineering priority. In the church, such a governance stands in blatant discrepancy with the image of the servant community whose life is risked, constantly, resiliently, for the sake of the renewal of the life of the world. In the church, to put it another way, such a managerial mentality capitalizes the worldliness of the church. The church becomes more conformed in this world where the church is most preoccupied in the maintenance of the ecclesial fabric.[24]

In 1973 a convocation was organized by the Berkeley Center at Yale around the question, "Does America Need a Barmen Declaration?" This took place at the time of great confusion when the Watergate disclosures were being made in the midst of the turmoil of the Vietnam War. The scandal of the Nixon administration was revealed in its corruption and its idolatrous and arrogant claims to power. Stringfellow summed up the question of the convocation by saying that the American churches did not possess at that time the moral authority to make such a confession.

This, then, was the position to which he had come. But Stringfellow by no means relented. In 1975 he called for an Episcopal Church in Exile. The presenting issue was the controversial ordination of women to the priesthood in Philadelphia in 1974. The inability of the Episcopal Church to affirm these ordinations, together with the continuing acrimony, led Stringfellow to raise the question whether the church has the capability for significant change as a church faithful to the Gospel, able to respond affirmatively to the urgency of the Holy Spirit. He predicted that out of this situation would emerge a new church within the church, a confessing movement, an extempore church embodying the change refused by the official church, a church in exile. And he declared this to be in all likelihood an ecumenical phenomenon already happening.

Though patient, by 1979 his patience had run out following the failure of the Denver General Convention to deal substantively with the several issues facing the church. This occasioned the famous "Open Letter," parts of which have been cited above. In the event, Stringfellow's chiding of the Presiding Bishop did not have the desired outcome. Bishop Allin did not resign. And little has changed. But Stringfellow's witness will not be neglected. As we consider our twilight civilization and the problematic destiny of America, Stringfellow assists us to see the possibilities of transformation and transfiguration.

At about this time, Stringfellow developed what I have called a transforming utopian vision of Christian worship as witness, of Eucharist as political action. In a sermon preached at the Episcopal Peace Fellowship Eucharist in Denver on September 7, 1979, just prior to the meeting of the General Convention of the Episcopal Church, he developed this vision. He proclaimed the Eucharist feast as rebuking and exorcising the demonic powers which were distorting and disturbing the common institutional life in church and commonwealth. Eucharist is the political action of the church, he proclaimed. It is a political manifesto that the Word of God reigns now; and it stands over against every power that contests and challenges the sovereignty of the Word of God in history. It is an emancipation from death; it beseeches the judgment of the Word of God in which the reign of Christ will be vindicated and all will be made accountable to the life of the whole of creation.[25] It is this transforming and transfiguring vision, I believe, which went beyond the limits and failures of common law and of canon law in ordering chaos and upholding justice. This spirit animates his book, *The Politics of Spirituality,*[26] as his final bequest. We have here a sort of Maccabean insurgency casting down the abomination of desolation and restoring the emblems of the one true Holy God in its place to the purifying of the life of the nation.

In June, 1985, I wrote as an editorial in the *St. Luke's Journal* the following:

> Bill Stringfellow was possibly the outstanding Episcopalian of this generation. Theologian, moralist, advocate, critic, his personal commitment to Christ and his keen perception into the heart of issues was inspiriting and edifying. His defense of the Philadelphia women ordinands and his defense of Bishop Pike were entirely appropriate, apposite, clarifying, and salutary. His impassioned opposition to cant was invigorating and inspiring. His willingness to call untruth into question supported the rest of us in our struggle with truth. His theological work and his prophetic life are unmatchable contributions to our Church and to its life. We who knew him, through his influence or through his work, are less impoverished for his own self-giving.[27]

NOTES

1 William Stringfellow, "Christian Vocation and the Legal Profession," *The Church Review* XVI:5 (April 1958), 3 ff.

2 Bill Wylie-Kellermann, *A Keeper of the Word* (Grand Rapids, Michigan: William B. Eerdmans Publishing, 1994), 33-35, 41-45.

3 William Stringfellow, "The Christian Lawyer as a Churchman," *Vanderbilt Law Review* 10 (August 1957), 964.

4 Robert N. Bellah, et al., *Habits of the Heart: Individualism and Commitment in American Life*, (New York: Harper and Row, 1986).

5 William Stringfellow, "Christian Faith and the American Lawyer," *Federation News* (May-August 1957), 79-81.

6 William Stringfellow, "Law, Polity, and the Reunion of the Church," *Ecumenical Review* XIII:3 (April 1961), 287 ff.

7 William Stringfellow, "The Crisis of Confidence and Ethics in the Legal Profession," *Capital University Law Review,* volume 9.

8 William Stringfellow, *My People Is the Enemy* (New York: Holt, Rinehart and Winston, 1964), 3.

9 Ibid., chapter 3.

10 Ibid., 37-38.

11 William Stringfellow, "Poverty, Law and the Ethics of Society," *North Dakota Law Review* 41 (1964-65), vi ff.

12 William Stringfellow, "Christianity, Poverty and the Practice of the Law," *Harvard Law School Bulletin* (June 1959), 66 ff.

13 Stringfellow, *My People Is the Enemy,* 38.

14 William Stringfellow and Anthony Towne, *The Bishop Pike Affair* (New York: Harper and Row, 1967), 116-17.

15 Ibid., 125.

16 Ibid., 118-19.

17 William Stringfellow, *The Witness* (September 1975), 5.

18 William Stringfellow, "An Open Letter to the Presiding Bishop," *The Witness* 63:1 (January 1980), 10.

19 John M. Gessell, editorial, *St. Luke's Journal of Theology* 20:4 (September 1977), 243-45.

20 Dean M. Kelley, "A Primer for Pastors," *Christianity and Crisis* 37:7 (May 2, 1977), 86-92.

21 William Stringfellow, *An Ethic for Christians and Other Aliens in a Strange Land* (Waco, Texas: Word Books, 1973); *Conscience and Obedience: The Politics of Romans 13 and Revelation 13 in the Light of the Second Coming* (Waco, Texas: Word Books, 1977).

22 William Stringfellow and Anthony Towne, *Suspect Tenderness* (New York: Holt, Rinehart and Winston, 1971).

23 Stringfellow, *An Ethic for Christians and Other Aliens in a Strange Land,* 84-86.

24 Stringfellow, "An Open Letter to the Presiding Bishop," 10-11.

25 William Stringfellow, sermon excerpts, *Episcopal Peace News* (Advent 1979), 1.

26 William Stringfellow, *The Politics of Spirituality* (Louisville, Kentucky: Westminster Press, 1984), especially chapter 3.

27 John M. Gessell, "William Stringfellow," *St. Luke's Journal of Theology* 28:3 (June 1985), 163.

STRINGFELLOW'S LEGACY TO LAWYERS
Resist the Profession[1]

ANDREW W. McTHENIA, JR.

William Stringfellow was always a stranger in a strange land. During his lifetime he was treated by mainstream communities as are most prophets in America; that is, he was viewed askance or entirely disregarded. Now, some ten years after his death, there seems to be something of a Stringfellow revival afoot. I am hopeful and at the same time apprehensive, because we have an uncanny ability to muffle the voices of our prophets in the cloak of nostalgia. We have done it with Martin Luther King. Few remember how King was marginalized when his opposition to the Vietnam War and his escalating campaign against economic injustice in America were perceived as genuine threats to the administration of President Lyndon Johnson. Almost no one remembers that he was murdered after spending the day on a picket line in a strike considered by the powers to be "illegal."

Yet Stringfellow might just survive efforts to make him respectable. Those venues which would normally be expected to grind the sharp edges from a prophetic voice and render it "safe"—universities and the mainline church—are themselves in serious disarray. There is no longer an "imperial" voice which can effectively silence voices from the margin. Many of those mainstream communities which never fully received Stringfellow now seem to be unraveling and groping for a mode of discourse that leaves space for a prophetic spirituality. And Stringfellow's voice is as clear as ever. It is a voice which demands a rejuvenation of community, personal responsibility, and economic justice. In short, it summons us now in the closing years of the second millennium, just as it did during his lifetime, to a renewed humanity.

There has always been something paradoxical about Stringfellow. While he was not much accepted in mainstream communities, he had a large following in communities of resistance—Sojourners, Jonah House, and Catholic Worker communities—groups which resolutely challenge the establishment at every turn. His presence was also important to a group of oddball lawyers—coming from a profession which is the primary guardian of the establishment. Those sorts of paradoxes in Stringfellow's life confront us around every corner. One has the sense that he is watching as we round these corners and impishly recalling Thomas Merton's famous line: "Like Jonah himself I find myself traveling toward my destiny in the belly of a paradox."

I am one of those oddball lawyers whose life was and continues to be affected by Stringfellow. While, on the surface, the issues I face as an academic living a life in the law seem very different from those which confronted Stringfellow in East Harlem, I know deep down that those same old powers and principalities are at work threatening to derail me in the struggle to live out my vocation.

Perhaps Stringfellow's major legacy to all of us who are lawyers is to be on guard, to resist the seductive claims of the legal profession. Stringfellow was always wary lest the powers of the profession would overtake him, and that awareness developed early while he was in law school. Interestingly one of his early meditations on vocation written shortly after he graduated from the Harvard Law School reflected the tension between the demands of the legal profession and his sense of vocation. And it was a tension that never eased for him. In the last years of his life he expressed it this way: "I continue to be haunted by the ironic impression that I may have to renounce being a lawyer, the better to be an advocate."[2] How he lived out that tension is an important story of resistance.

The legal profession in America was—at the time Stringfellow entered law school—even more closely knit than it is now. It was marked by well-defined boundaries and was extremely hierarchical in nature. Many things help insure these distinctions in the profession; and among them the place of one's legal education is not insignificant. For more than a century, the Harvard Law School has been at or near the center of the legal culture in America.

There was, in the years following World War II, a symbiotic relationship between the world view of Harvard and the legal profession. Harvard was the citadel of legal process thinking. Law in action as envisioned by the legal process school was a search for shared principles in the social order. That philosophy rested on the assumption of an expanding and progressive social order in which the majority of the citizenry shared the same underlying values, values of Enlightenment rationalism—so-called neutral principles. Most crucial to this "process school" was a shared belief in the competency of institutions, particularly courts, to decide how questions of policy would be answered.

The trick of course was to uncover those underlying neutral principles. And that search was to be guided by courts. Judges were, by virtue of their training and station, uniquely suited for this detached philosopher king role. The nagging question of how there could be objective underlying values knitting the citizens of a liberal democracy—a system premised on a pluralistic subjectivity of values—was for a long time disregarded. However, it never fully disappeared.[3] This search for neutral principles left little room for asking whether the principles that undergird the law are all that neutral. Nor did it leave much room for asking questions about justice. Stringfellow, reflecting on his time at Harvard, put it this way: "I also thought, while I was in law school, that *justice* is a suitable topic for consideration in practically every course or specialization. Alas, it was seldom mentioned, and the term itself evoked ridicule, as if justice were a subject beneath the sophistication of lawyers."[4] And the search left *no* room for questions of faith or for questions about the relationship between faith and law.

The emphasis on the law's commitment to underlying rational values through process tended to deify existing social structures, particularly courts, and to elevate to a priestly caste the legal academy, which was charged with nurturing the rule-of-law values of objectivity, stability, and predictability. The profession—with its faith in Enlightenment rationalism insured by its trusted gatekeeper, the legal academy—proceeded as if there had never been any connection between the western legal tradition and faith. And that secular seminary known as the Harvard Law School was the primary defender of the faith of the law's commitment to rationalism.

The nexus between law and theology was simply disregarded as American law continued on a fiercely secular path. As a result of that process, law students came to see the connection between theology and law as mostly a dis-connection; and, to the extent they considered that there remained any nexus at all, they thought first, not of theology, but of law. Whatever vestigial memories of faith communities the students might have brought with them to law school were generally transformed into notions of alien enterprises threatening the constituted order of autonomous liberalism. In the legal academy, religion was simply irrelevant and, therefore, cabined off into the safe status of merely "private and subjective." The irony of all this was not lost on Stringfellow. He intuited that the faith in judges to uncover underlying values was itself a religion—the religion of the intellectual. It is not so surprising that he considered himself a stranger at the Harvard Law School.

Most legal academics in mid-twentieth century would not accept that there could be small insular communities separate and apart from the larger *polis*. It made even less sense to think of such a community centering its life in worship. To the extent that theological belief was acknowledged as a reality, it was an abstraction, not as something which could assert an intellectual and spiritual discipline different from and beyond that imposed by society at large.

Stringfellow simply rejected the strain of Enlightenment thinking that would separate the world into public and private spheres, defining reality as that which is objective and empirically knowable. There is an arrogant strain of modernism which seeks to prohibit discussion of views that present a truly radical challenge to modernity's established structures of thought. And certainly liberal Protestantism, having been seduced by modernity, was in no position to pick up the challenge. Stringfellow was resisting this established structure when he insisted that any conversation about theology and law must begin with grace. To do otherwise would be unfaithful. He saw what many of us often miss, that the gods of modernity are so well disguised that often we do not see that the altars are in fact the structures of the imposed mode of discourse.[5]

It is not, as some have argued, that Stringfellow thought that law was nothing but a tool of oppression or, as others have maintained, that he was unconcerned with justice. He saw law as necessary, even as a gift from God. And he spent his life in the struggle for justice. His last book, *The Politics of Spirituality*, written literally as he was dying, is an unremitting plea to continue the struggle for justice.[6] But law, like all other powers and principalities, is fallen. Law is one means, the primary one, that a modern liberal democracy has to safeguard itself and the promised freedom of its members. Stringfellow never denied the value or the necessity of law for those purposes. But many liberal academic lawyers insisted on going further.[7] They asserted that not only is law necessary to preserve the peace treaty of a liberal democracy; it is in fact the source of our values. Law is that which gives expression to those "objective" values in our culture. These lawyers saw a large role for law, linking the reality of the present with the world as we imagine it should be. Law for them had an almost transcendent quality.

Stringfellow resolutely rejected the notion that law is somehow transformative. He knew that law not only had no saving power, but that it was itself a power and principality. He saw law at best as a boundary marking the "isness" of the present—a world in which we live as sinners saved by grace—from an imagined but not yet present world—the Eschaton, a world in which we will all rest as sisters and brothers under the fig tree. The law is incapable of taking us to that future. There is a constant tension between law and grace. To surrender that tension was in his view apostasy. We often do it because we want a *via media*, a synthesis; we think we can by dint of our own effort make law benign. Stringfellow thought that it is our own hubris that leads us to think we can "fix" the fallen powers.

> Americans particularly persevere in belaboring the illusion that at least some institutions are benign and viable and within human direction or can be rendered so by discipline or reform or revolution or displacement.[8]

He was unceasing in his insistence that this notion would lead to despair and devastate all hope for justice. And he was equally insistent that *only* the reality of the resurrection can replace this false optimism with genuine hope. Prophetic discernment, which is the life work for all of us, involves sensitivity to the Word of God, which is even now breaking into and transfiguring history.

It is the community of the baptized—the generic church—that has a vision of what the future under God's reign will be like. Baptism creates a people dedicated to the vision of a world redeemed. The discernment—about any matter whatever—that is given and exercised in that relationship is conscience. And conscience comes from God. It is the breaking in of the Holy Spirit into our lives and actions. Because it is the breaking in of the Holy Spirit, it is utterly unpredictable; and because it intrudes into the banality, the everydayness, the brokenness of this world, it is intensely political. The claim of conscience insists that the future will be on God's terms.[9] Conscience is a command breaking into the world of the unredeemed present that tells one what to do or not do in relation to the coming kingdom.[10] And because it is a living encounter between the baptized community and the Word of God, the exercise of conscience cannot be enclosed or evaluated by humans, by law, by custom, by the ethics of the culture, or by the state.[11]

And the claim of conscience always, not just on occasion but always, puts the believer in opposition to the status quo. Stringfellow, talking about the demoralization of America, spoke of living in resistance.

> It goes without saying . . . that in circumstances where moral decadence . . . becomes so pervasive in a nation, one can discern and identify maturity, conscience, and paradoxically, freedom in human beings only among those who are in conflict with the established order—those who are opponents of the status quo, those in rebellion against the system, those who are prisoners, resisters, fugitives, and victims. And only, by the same token, incidentally, can one postulate any ground of hope for a viable future for the United States.[12]

One issue that draws the line between Stringfellow and the liberal rule-of-law advocates is the law's resort to violence. Some of his admirers have criticized Stringfellow for failing to condemn absolutely the use of violence.[13] But I think he saw law more clearly and realistically than do most of us. The reality is that violence and pain and death are a part of this fallen world,[14] a reality that one cannot avoid on the streets of East Harlem.

> Slowly I learned something which folk indigenous to the ghetto know: namely, that the power and purpose of death are incarnated in institutions and structures, procedures and regimes— Consolidated Edison or the Department of Welfare, the Mafia or the police, the Housing Authority or the social work bureaucracy, the hospital system or the banks, liberal philanthropy or corporate real estate speculation. In the wisdom of the people of the East Harlem neighborhood, such principalities are identified as demonic powers because of the relentless and ruthless dehumanization which they cause.[15]

And this is the world in which law as a principality operates. Although defenders of the rule-of-law ideal do not like to admit it, law is in bondage to violence. We lawyers often try to avoid that reality by talking of the rule of law, of due process, and, on occasion, of justice. But law remains in theological terms a fallen power. If it sees itself threatened, law will resort to violence. Whether the resort to violence is of the dramatic sort exercised when the economic and political order of the liberal democratic state in America was threatened by Mormonism[16] in the nineteenth century or whether it is of the sort exercised when a defendant is gagged in the courtroom because she will not obey the judge's order to be silent, one cannot blink from the reality that Robert Cover captured so powerfully: "Were the inhibition against violence perfect, law would be unnecessary; were it not capable of being overcome . . . law would not be possible."[17]

Resistance communities and political prisoners in jails and prisons of America have never had any illusions about that. No matter how many layers of bureaucracy separate the Supreme Court from the executioner, it is the voice of law that pulls the switch. The fact that law must and does resort to violence does not mean that it is evil, but merely that it is fallen. That is a lawyer's way of saying that the law has no saving power. Stringfellow himself experienced the law as an aggressor when he was indicted for harboring Father Dan Berrigan. And that led him to wonder:

> . . . if the law's aggressions against blacks are admitted and, for the sake of maintaining the illusion that institutions are or can be made truly viable, it is suggested that the law in America remains nonetheless viable for white citizens or that there are in fact racially identifiable two legal systems, then the most crucial issue respecting the supposed viability of principalities emerges. If the American legal system seems viable for me and other white Americans but it is not so for citizens who are black, or for any others, then *how* as the dual commandment would ask, in the *name of humanity, can it be affirmed as viable for me or for any human being?*[18]

In a world redeemed, there will be no violence, and Stringfellow knew that. That is why his life is properly characterized as a testament of hope. He did not try to evade the tension; instead he lived into it fully. And the vocational call for all of us is to live humanly in this fallen world and proclaim by acts large and small—mostly small— that violence will be unacceptable when the powers are brought into conformity with God's plan.

To live in resistance to the more idolatrous claims of the legal system frees those of us who live lives in the law to recognize our clients as gifts to be cherished. And also to know that our work of justice is a form of prayer and praise.

NOTES

1 An abbreviated version of this essay was published in *Faith and Freedom,* an Australian journal commemorating William Stringfellow's life and work.

2 William Stringfellow, "A Lawyer's Work," *Christian Legal Society Quarterly* 3 (1982): 17, 19.

3 See E. Mensch, "The History of Mainstream Legal Thought," in David Karys, ed., *The Politics of Law*, 32.

4 William Stringfellow, *A Simplicity of Faith: My Experience in Mourning*, (Nashville: Abingdon Press, 1982), 126-127.

5 Sanford Levinson, "Religious Language and the Public Square," *Harvard Law Review* 105 (1992): 2061.

6 William Stringfellow, *The Politics of Spirituality*, (Philadelphia: Westminster Press, 1984).

7 See Owen M. Fiss, "The Supreme Court, 1978 Term—Forward: The Forms of Justice," *Harvard Law Review* 93 (1979). See also idem, "The Law Regained," *Cornell Law Review* 76 (1989): 245, 249: "Adjudication is nothing more than or less than a social institution for interpreting and enforcing our public values."

8 William Stringfellow, *An Ethic for Christians and Other Aliens in a Strange Land,* (Waco, Texas: Word Books, 1973), 83.

9 William Stringfellow and Anthony Towne, *Suspect Tenderness: The Ethics of the Berrigan Witness,* (New York: Holt, Rinehart and Winston, 1971), 97-103.

10 Stringfellow, *An Ethic for Christians and Other Aliens in a Strange Land,* 138-43.

11 Stringfellow and Towne, *Suspect Tenderness*, 97-103.

12 Stringfellow, *An Ethic for Christians and Other Aliens in a Strange Land,* 31.

13 Walter Wink, "Stringfellow on the Powers," in Andrew W. McThenia, Jr., ed., *Radical Christian and Exemplary Lawyer: A Festschrift Honoring William Stringfellow* (Grand Rapids, Michigan: William B. Eerdmans Publishing, 1995), 27-30.

14 Robert M. Cover, "Violence and the Word," *Yale Law Journal* 95 (1986): 1601.

15 William Stringfellow, *Instead of Death* (New York: Seabury Press, 1976), 5.

16 For a discussion of the violence of the liberal state against the Mormons in the nineteenth century, see Stanley Hauerwas, Sanford Levinson, and Mark V. Tushnet, "Faith in the Republic: A Frances

Lewis Law Center Conversation," *Washington and Lee Law Review* 45 (1988): 493-94.

17 Cover, "Violence and the Word," 1613.

18 Stringfellow, *An Ethic for Christians and Other Aliens in a Strange Land,* 85-86.

HARLEM AND ESCHATON
Stringfellow's Theological Homes[1]

GARY COMMINS

When William Stringfellow graduated from Harvard Law School in 1956, he went to do legal work with the East Harlem Protestant Parish, an ecumenical experiment in urban ministry. In 1967—because Stringfellow was ill but also because he and Anthony Towne wanted to find a place where they might expand their ministry of hospitality and deepen their monastic vocation—they moved to Block Island, off the coast of Rhode Island. Following the custom of the island, they named their household. Following their theological bent, they named it Eschaton.

These two places—Harlem and Eschaton—shed light on every aspect of Stringfellow's thought: his theology and ethics, his emphases on incarnation and eschatology, his insights into the power of death, the principalities and powers, church and state, and the Word of God. In them lie the deepest roots of his alienation from church and state. These two "villages"—one an "occupied territory," the other an underdeveloped area ripe for exploitation—were his theological homes.[2]

Stringfellow probably would have agreed with the Orthodox contention that only one who prays, who writes from an experience of God, could be a theologian. He certainly insisted that a theologian had to write from an experience of the world. Like Karl Barth, Stringfellow abhorred abstract religious speculation. Daily occurrences and ordinary people were the most profound source of theology.[3] Biography and autobiography were, like parables, pregnant with meaning. This, he explained, was congruent with the incarnation. The stories he tells throughout his sixties' books, his Harlem books, were not illustrations leading to a theoretical conclusion. They were the primary subject matter for—and inspiration of—his theological reflection, the dirt—filled with God's spirit—he used to create and mold his theology.

His descriptions of poverty in the opening pages of *My People is the Enemy* are reminiscent of the works of Dorothy Day.[4] Both of them made the poor the plumbline and prism of their theology. Day lovingly detailed the sights, smells, and psychological storms of poverty etched in each creased face. Stringfellow detailed the cruelty of poverty, replacing brittle, fearful middle-class stereotypes with wounded yet well-rounded human beings. As Day loathed "telescopic philanthropy," suburban charity untainted by the odor of destitution, Stringfellow disdained telescopic theology, scholastic work apart from biography, away from Harlem, "aloof from life."[5]

Critics scolded Stringfellow for a lack of training in academic theology, a lack of technical discipline, a lack of scholarly detachment. Some preferred his social criticism and political analysis to his "theological mumblings."[6] But in his mind, a living theology could not be clinically, surgically, or artificially separated from social criticism, political analysis, or emotional engagement. It was as if they were Siamese quadruplets sharing one spinal cord and one heart. His foreword to *Dissenter in a Great Society* may have provided rubrics for all of his books when he said that it included "spontaneous reactions to certain contemporary happenings, sometimes in indignation, sometimes in grief, in frustration, in hope, in depression, sometimes—I suppose—in idealism, sometimes in apprehension, sometimes in anguish."[7]

Sharing the life of the poor—the vast majority of the human race—was a way "to honor the incarnation," a way to be "home." Writing from Harlem precluded the luxury of dispassionate discourse about the high-handedness of the Great Society or the institutionalized pillaging of his neighborhood.[8] Theological assertions had to emerge from, and be tested against, the world "as it is." The truths revealed in Scripture, he asserted, were confirmed by real life. He considered himself as an "empirical theologian."[9]

While Carter Heyward rightly described Stringfellow's theology as "vintage" neo-orthodox, his theology was crucified and born again by his encounter with the daily realities of his neighbors and clients in Harlem. Writing in an academic atmosphere in the fifties, Stringfellow wrote in the lexicon of the Fall, sin and redemption. Only in Harlem did he begin to use the word "death" to speak of evil. In Harlem, he first saw the principalities—institutions, bureaucracies, utilities, businesses, professions—devouring their human prey.[10]

Harlem cried out for justice, but Stringfellow never developed a formal theodicy. His physical pain, Towne's sudden death, and Harlem's endless plight led him to ask "why?" less often than the psalmists' other lament: "how long?" While in Harlem, he found solace in Christ's descent to Hell—the logical and final extension of the incarnation—where the power of death was militant and matured to perfection. Through the incarnation, Christ shared all suffering; even in Hell, Christ triumphed. Resurrection prevailed in Harlem as it did in Hell.[11]

From Eschaton, he reported that he had read "the defeat of the saints" (Revelation 13:7) a thousand times, a repeated act revealing his own puzzlement and a spiritual battle with the questions "why?" and "how long?" In counterpoint, he probably proclaimed of the triumph of the Word hundreds of times. The saints were defeated; the Word triumphed. This paradox was, in effect, his theodicy.[12] Theodicy was resolved by the Word made flesh, Christ's descent to hell, and the eschatological Judge who already reigned.

For Stringfellow, the incarnation was not a scandal of particularity, but the surprise of ubiquity. Jesus Christ was an "illustrious instance" of the incarnation of the Word, but the Word was "implanted" in all of history, inherent in all creation. Jesus' ministry was filled with signs of his "authority over death"—healing the sick, calming the storm, casting out demons, eating with sinners, cleansing the temple, raising the dead, bearing the Cross. In the same fashion, the Word held universal and eternal dominion over creation that would be finalized at the end, when the Word acted as judge over death.[13]

Stringfellow found incarnational theology in eschatological writings and eschatological theology in the Feast of the Incarnation. The book of Revelation, he claimed, celebrated "incarnational theology." In turn, the traditional manger scene was a portrait of the time to come, "peace on earth" an eschatological utterance warning of judgment and inviting all nations to repent.[14]

Always and everywhere, incarnation and eschatology were linked, intensifying the significance of every moment and every person, adding to the intensity of Stringfellow's writings. Each day had the dignity of the first and last days, as if it were the only day, "as if today and eternity were one": "Eden and the Fall, Jerusalem and Babylon, Eschaton and Apocalypse converge here and now." Time itself was a product of the fall, so worship celebrated the "transcendence of time in time." Eschatology was not "some nebulous promise" encouraging fatalistic passivity, but a hope "embodied and verified in the transfiguration of the common life of human beings in society here and now."[15]

Several friends described Stringfellow's relationship with Towne as "monastic," their home as a place of retreat. Stringfellow shared theological homes with Thomas Merton who worked briefly in Harlem and had a more traditional monastic vocation. Merton emphasized the importance of the vision of the Desert, an ability to see the world more clearly for having "left it," and a "Desert Protest," an eschatological witness against powers that deform human life. Stringfellow's vision, awakened in Harlem, was attuned by Eschaton. The monastic lives of Stringfellow and Merton had the same theological result: their writings on sin and the Fall gradually gave birth to an emphasis on the restoration of creation.[16]

There is a distinct shift in Stringfellow's writings around 1970. Incarnation and eschatology interact in all of his books, but his physical move to Block Island marked a theological absorption with eschatology. Geographically, he had changed villages. Historically, the paternalistic Great Society prepared the way for the malicious Watergate State. Personally, he endured the ordeal of a near-death experience that left him in constant jeopardy and chronic pain. The words "alien" and "dissenter" overlap in his Harlem books until, at Eschaton, "dissenter" disappeared and "alien" gained pre-eminence. As innately foreign as Harlem was to mainstream society, Eschaton made him even stranger to his strange land.

In Harlem—the place most obviously subject to death—he witnessed the Word's victory already taking place. The Desert Fathers had described the monk's cell as both the furnace of Babylon and a pillar of cloud. Stringfellow's "cell" was Harlem where he felt God's tragic absence and mysterious presence. Eschatological hope, like a thick cloud, was "recurrently foreshadowed and empirically witnessed in events taking place now, and all the time, in the common history of persons and nations in this world."[17]

> Encircled by the manifoldness of death—the death so impatiently at work in my own body; the death so militant in my own country; the death so idolized by my own race; the death which seems to be the moral sovereign in the world; the death incarnate in all existence everywhere . . . . I felt alive: very much alive: never more alive.[18]

In Harlem, the signs of death were everywhere—poverty, racism, addiction, unemployment, disease, oppression. Every estrangement, alienation, and loss of identity anywhere was a taste of death. In a sense, Stringfellow's chronic physical pain was his own personal taste of the Fall, a life in perpetual danger in an era of everlasting crisis in which all relationships were distorted and all creatures disoriented. Harlem, for him, was "a symbol of *every* aggression of death and of *every* triumph over death."[19]

Commentators claimed that Stringfellow was "fixated" on death—Towne's, his own, death as a social force and a cosmic power. They barely missed the truth. In his chronicle of his "experience in mourning," Stringfellow observed that he could have allowed himself to grieve forever. If he had, "the power of death would not only have claimed Anthony in the grave but would also seize me." He refused to let "grief define my living." As he had hinted in his foreword to *Dissenter in a Great Society*, this was his spiritual battle—in Harlem, during the Nixon regime, with church and state. In a world being crushed between the jaws of death, grief was Stringfellow's daily mouthful of ashes and his awful temptation. His ability to transcend grief drew others—chilled in the same shadow of death, wrestling an invisible, suffocating sorrow—to him.[20]

Harlem's citizens introduced Stringfellow to the principalities and powers which, he believed, consigned themselves—without exception—to the power of death. Death worked militantly through universities, corporations, labor unions, political institutions, businesses, and technology. As he once unveiled Billy Graham's nostalgia for pastoral America as an avoidance of urban realism, he later noted that his own view of the principalities so transcended Reinhold Niebuhr's comprehension of coercible corporate power that he likened Niebuhr's quaintness to Graham's. The principalities were universally "predatory," consumed with their own survival, compelled to invert creation as they seized dominion over the human race. Niebuhr found corporate power difficult to steer; Stringfellow insisted that the powers were creatures with lives and wills of their own. Whether perceived as benign, malign, or benevolent, Plato's republic, Constantine's empire, Rousseau's social contract, Jeffersonian democracy, Marx's classless society, the free enterprise system, and world government served death. Niebuhr had little hope for easy change; Stringfellow had none. Christians were to call the principalities to repent and serve God, a vocation they had abandoned at the Fall. The church was to be the principality which, by its repentance, foreshadowed the final perfection of all principalities.[21]

While Stringfellow named dozens of principalities and sometimes focused on the legal and medical professions, two of the powers—state and church—dominated his theology and embodied the conflict between Fall and eschaton, despair and hope, subservience to death and freedom through the Word. He measured the incarnate realities of church and state against their eschatological destinies, and found them sorely wanting.[22]

While in Harlem, he stressed the importance of the city; from "a step off America," he focused on the state. Surprisingly, he did not call the - city a principality. Rather, it was occupied and terrorized by principalities. Every city was Babylon, a place of death, "the epitome of the Fall"; every city was also the City of Salvation, "a sign of the Eschaton."[23]

The state was another matter. On occasion he called it a "constellation" of principalities; most often, he deemed it the principality *par excellence.* Saying in *Conscience and Obedience* that he interpreted the U.S. through Romans 13 and Revelation 13 was another way of stating that he wrote from Harlem and Eschaton. Neither gave a favorable view of the twentieth-century American empire. Harlem saw the state as a kind of self-justifying rapist. From Eschaton, every social reform (real or imagined) paled in comparison to the final reconciliation; every social problem was revealed as blasphemy.[24]

As an empirical theologian—and an attorney—Stringfellow seemed to delight in detailing the sins that pockmarked the U.S. Property rights superseded human rights. The idolatrous Protestant work ethic had become a wealth ethic, making poverty a sin, and the poor sinners. White supremacy, encompassing blatant racism and liberal paternalism, was the dominant American ideology. The spiritual roots of the Vietnam War lay in chattel slavery and genocidal policies against Native Americans. Violence propelled the national economy and was praised for its power to sanctify and save.[25]

While noting the grim consistencies of racism, violence, and greed in American history, Stringfellow believed that the U.S. had entered a dark age in the second half of the twentieth century.[26] Here lay one of the paradoxes in his thinking: the state had always been an instrument of death; the state had become an instrument of death.

Stringfellow expressed the other chief paradox in his theology of the state in two actions toward Richard Nixon. Before Watergate, in the spring of 1972, he called for Nixon's impeachment. Months later, the night before Nixon's second inauguration, he offered a solemn prayer for Nixon's exorcism. Some might construe the second action as a rhetorical escalation of the first, but the two actions make opposing claims. In calling for impeachment, he asserted that an individual was free to choose: limit the evil of the state or become a sorry serf. He called Nixon "a barbarian." His conduct, in concert with Henry Kissinger, was "distinguished by violence, savagery, lust, malevolence, avarice, and an overwhelming contempt for human life." Yet theirs was a "Faustian story." Their own humanity had been devoured by the principality they served. Nixon was not only a criminal; he was a "pathetic" prisoner in dire need of exorcism.[27] Stringfellow tried to correct those who vilified Nixon as if he were the power of death itself. Nixon had merely cooperated with the power of death with a perverse purity that eroded positive cultural values and brought the nation's violent self-destructiveness to a bizarre fruition.

When it became fashionable in liberal religious circles to call for a new Barmen Declaration, Stringfellow carefully discerned the historical differences between Germany in the thirties and the U.S. in the seventies. Yet he also applied the book of Revelation's Babylon parable to both. The Babylon parable, he believed, always applied. Empirically speaking, *every* nation was Babylon, claiming to be Jerusalem, the city of hope, the chosen people of God. Every nation sought to usurp God's power and seduce human loyalty. Like all nations, Germany in the thirties and the U.S. in the seventies were Babylon, proud towers pretending to reign while unconsciously preparing for their demise when the Second Advent consummated the work born in the First. On that day, all political authorities would be destroyed by the Word, and Christ's reign would bear its full and final fruit.[28]

The state was the archetypal principality—using death as its only moral sanction, exercising dominion over humanity in the service of death. Stringfellow's evolution from law student to social reformer to eschatological theologian was complete. Once an advocate for progressive social change, he came to believe that reform was a dead-end delusion. The state would not respond to the social gospel's moral persuasions, nor to neo-orthodox coercion. The state was immune to reform.[29]

Stringfellow's writings, it was said, made H. R. Niebuhr's "Christ against Culture" model the *only* viable Christian view. To him, this was not an abstract theological discernment; it was grounded in empiricism and eschatology. Niebuhr's other options made no sense in Stringfellow's two villages. He asserted that the most significant christological title was "Lord," a word exploding with political implications. Christ exercised Lordship over defiant and blasphemous nations. As a principality, there was absolutely no hope for America. Yet, paradoxically (again), Stringfellow hoped that the U.S. would confess its blasphemy. If it did not repent now, it *would* do so at "the time of the judgment of the Word of God." In Harlem, he observed that no nation would serve God until the end of history. What he saw from Eschaton confirmed his position.[30]

If the state met his expectations, the church frustrated his hopes. Most of Stringfellow's pre-Harlem ministry took place within the ecumenical movement. The ecumenism of the East Harlem Protestant Parish may have attracted him as much as urban ministry. The church, he said, witnessed to the world by its internal unity—a sign of the coming reconciliation—and by exposing the state's pretensions, calling the state to turn from the power of death to the Word of God. In the sixties, he stressed organic cohesion. In the seventies, the witness to the state almost eclipsed his concern for ecumenism.[31]

Stringfellow described the church's call in his first book: it was the Body of Christ living in the world on behalf of the world, discerning and celebrating God's presence here. The deepest issues of faith were Harlem's issues: poverty, racism, estrangement, unemployment, prison. When the church advocated for victims and worked with outcasts, it fulfilled its vocation as an image and "embassy" of the eschaton. A church that did not care for the world did not care for Jesus.[32]

The church was judged from both Harlem and the eschaton. In the fifties and sixties, denominations orchestrated an exodus from inner cities. When churches had not fled in fear, they conflated bourgeois values with Christian faith. Their late entry into the civil rights movement coexisted with financial investments in institutional racism; pious words of peace never prevented churches from profiting from war. Harlem saw the church as "imperious, condescending, unknowing, indifferent, unloving, [and] hypocritical." The church was constantly obsessed with "churchly housekeeping, the nurture of religiosity, and miscellaneous soothsaying." Stringfellow's litmus test for the church was to see if it were "eschatologically ready."[33] It seemed that it had not yet recovered from the First Advent.

Given that the church was supposed to call the state to repent, the Constantinian "accommodation" sickened Stringfellow. It made as much sense as a deal between John the Baptist and Herod.[34] The church abandoned its witness and bartered blessings on American wealth and power in exchange for a place in the American kingdom. The church in the U.S., instead of being an example to principalities, had become their "handmaiden," making itself "among the most menial, manipulated, and degraded vassals of the power of death."[35]

Stringfellow's disillusionment with the empirical reality of the church never extinguished his hope. He did not advocate a non-institutional church or envision an invisible one. The church—enacting its true vocation—was "episodic in history," "visible here and there and now and then." There were occasional incarnations—in a congregation in Harlem, in the struggle against racism, in denunciations of war and annunciations of alternatives to violence.[36] In amorphous bodies and odd events, the church fulfilled its vocation, witnessing against the state, defying the principalities, clinging to the Word.

In Stringfellow's eyes, the church needed to become more like his beloved circus which was "an eschatological scene" and a model of Christian life. Circus performers faced, ridiculed, and defeated the power of death walking on the high wire, facing fierce beasts, being shot from cannons. In its sideshows, the circus embodied the diversity of humanity and creation. In taming wild animals, it incarnated the restoration of human dominion that had been lost at the Fall and would be renewed at the End. The circus parodied frenetic and enervating pursuits of happiness, exposed the folly of the powerful, and heralded a new reign.[37]

Since the church failed to be exemplary while the state succeeded as a ruthless archetype, the Christian was left to search for rudimentary tools to overcome the power of death. Stringfellow's ethical non-system proclaimed freedom, conscience, discernment, and resistance. He disdained ethical systems as he rejected speculative theology. There were no divine precedents or eternal principles. All the Christian needed were two feet planted in the world and a heart set on the age to come. Stringfellow's statement that there were "no disincarnate issues" makes his ethics bear some similarity to situation, contextual, utilitarian, and Bonhoeffer's obedience ethics. But Stringfellow had a unique emphasis. Conversion meant complete freedom from anxiety about one's justification, eternal well-being, or the Word's final triumph. The Christian was free "now" from bondage to idolatry, conformity to the world, and the fear of death. Free from second-guessing one's actions and oneself, free to transcend self-interest, free to act without calculating the consequences until "judged by God's mercy," the Christian was free "to live in hope while awaiting the Judgment." Ethics were always eschatological since both were preoccupied with "hope in its relationship to judgment." Ethics were an "eschatological anticipation . . . of the judgment of the Word of God in history." "Every conscientious act [is] historic," every decision incarnational. The "already/not yet" of the reign of God meant freedom now to trust in mercy at the end.[38]

Freed from the fear of death and a terror of God, the Christian could use the gifts of the Spirit, especially the gifts of discernment. In order to obey God, the Christian needed to discern the signs of the times: death within social reforms, the eschatological connotations of contemporary life, salvation during the Fall, the reality of resurrection where despair seems to reign. With the gift to discern spirits, the Christian could identify and utilize the powers given by the Holy Spirit to conquer death.[39]

As the eschatological trumpets in Stringfellow's writings drowned out all other music, an undertone of resistance became unmistakable. The present was determined by the End. Biblical living meant watching for advent; biblical politics anticipating Christ as judge. Thomas Merton, seeking to clarify what he valued in the world (and what the world hated), once imagined a bomb that would destroy toys, tools, books, gardens, works of art, and musical instruments, while preserving flags, weapons, and straitjackets. Stringfellow treasured the things that affirmed life: dancing, singing, music, painting, poetry, opera, ballet, literature, kite-flying, parades, and the circus.[40] These were tastes of the eschaton in the present, foretastes to live by and live on until the End. His life at Eschaton, literally filled with representations of the circus, was intended as a witness of hope and joy, healing the grief that gnawed at those who saw the principalities leeching the life out of people, neighborhoods, cities, and the nation.

In *A Second Birthday*, Stringfellow cryptically relates a consequence of his Lazarus-like brush with death. His loss of weight and physical attractiveness led someone to reject him.[41] He bemoaned the personal loss, and grieved at the person's failure in abandoning him when his life was in such peril.

Stringfellow endured many other rejections. He was dismissed as a "lay theologian," a freak for an ecclesiastical sideshow. Bishops in the Episcopal Church tried to prevent him from speaking in their dioceses. The General Convention received a resolution to censure him. Critics complained that his "iconoclasm" offended almost everyone, that his writings reeked of "paranoia," that he was a "prophet of doom." A former colleague wrote, "He was rude. He was ruthless. He was rigid. And he was right": a potent and obnoxious combination.[42]

His choice of words seemed calculated to make his writings singularly alienating. He not only called for Richard Nixon's impeachment and prayed for his exorcism, he sought an anathema against Ronald Reagan, and branded a whole nation—anxious to see itself as Zion—"Babylon." He considered the Union Theological Seminary an "enemy camp." He asked the Episcopal Church's Presiding Bishop to resign. He said that the General Convention was lost in interminable irrelevance, and accused the House of Bishops of "episodes of befuddlement, outbursts of hysteria, vainglorious indulgences, and prolonged lapses of incoherence." He had a talent for making enemies.[43]

Stringfellow, being an attorney, selected his words deliberately. In *The Bishop Pike Affair*, he denounced the absurdity of branding someone in the Episcopal Church a heretic, yet he accused the church—repeatedly—of heresy and apostasy, and the state of idolatry and blasphemy.[44] As he often noted, these words were not hyperbole. They were carefully crafted accusations of specific crimes against God. Thus, church and state often experienced him as an *accuser*.

Even his book titles described him as a dissenter, an enemy, and an alien. Throughout his writings he asserted that Christians always opposed every political and ecclesiastical status quo, since Christians gave their sole allegiance to the great reconciliation to come.[45]

"To be a Christian," he wrote, "is to receive and know and participate in the unconditional, extravagant, inexhaustible, expendable love of God for all that [God] has made and called into being." Few who felt the sting of Stringfellow's words discerned "love" at the heart of his writings. Yet, he wrote with a "grieving compassion," grief at the apparent victory of death in the world, compassion for all of its victims. He described himself as "the most passionate person" he knew. His passions found an endless supply of fuel in unbearable suffering and inexorable hope. The calling to which he was "disposed charismatically" was *advocacy*, taking up the causes of society's victims. He could not be an advocate without invoking the most powerful words he could find to accuse so many of so much.[46]

Asked in a sixties television interview if he had any hope, Stringfellow stunned the reporter when he replied that he did, in the Second Coming, which he prayed would come soon. Like John of Patmos, Stringfellow tried to write a "theology of hope" when isolated and surrounded by death. "The eschatological condition itself"— hope—enabled him to see the eschaton already at work in Harlem. When he wrote in Eschaton, he wrote—literally—from hope.[47]

In his last book, *The Politics of Spirituality*, Stringfellow said that he was convinced of a "realism grounded in the biblical insight into the fallenness of the whole of creation." Yet, just as the Cross is the gate into new life, realism itself was "the very threshold of hope."[48] Far more than his temperament, even more than his vocation to advocacy, the ground of Stringfellow's controversial nature was his rootedness in Harlem and Eschaton, realism and hope. The state, certainly, and the church, sadly, could not stand much of either one.

Because Harlem was home, his people were the enemy. Because Eschaton was home, he was an alien. These were the touchstones of his theology. While Stringfellow found much in Karl Barth's theological vocabulary to be congenial to his thinking, it was really Stringfellow's experience of suffering and hope, like that of John of Patmos, that gives power and lasting significance to his writings. If he had a theological mentor, it was John more than Karl. Stringfellow saw everything—death and the Word, church and state, principalities and Christian freedom, the whole world—from two villages, two islands, Harlem and Eschaton.

Stringfellow's home at Eschaton, it was said, became a "refuge for battered activists." His theology—a kind of written Eschaton— had the same function, providing shelter, anchoring hope not in political action but in the time to come. Like John of Patmos, he sustained faith with visions of hope in terrifying times. This, he said, was why people turned to the book of Revelation. This was why people—indignant, anguished, frustrated, and depressed—turned to him. In word and deed, his hope was like a well-stocked table in an empty, oppressive wilderness.[49]

Today, when hope seems a wisp, when principalities run amok, when so many feel so battered, when realism seems so gritty and tragic as to be indigestible by body or spirit, we need to revisit Stringfellow's villages and vision so that we, too, may not succumb to the temptation to make grief our way of life, so that we, too, may call an incarnational hope our home.

NOTES

1 An earlier version of this essay appeared in the *Anglican Theological Review*.

2 William Stringfellow, *A Second Birthday* (Garden City, New York: Doubleday, 1970), 18, 203; idem, *Dissenter in a Great Society: A Christian View of America in Crisis*, (New York: Holt, Rinehart and Winston, 1966), 20; idem, *A Simplicity of Faith: My Experience in Mourning* (Nashville: Abingdon Press, 1982), 94, 98-99.

3 Stringfellow, *A Simplicity of Faith*, 19-21; idem, *Count It All Joy* (Grand Rapids, Michigan: William B. Eerdmans Publishing, 1967), 54, 58; idem, "Harlem, Rebellion, and Resurrection," *The Christian Century* 87:45 (November 11, 1970), 1345; idem, *A Private and Public Faith* (Grand Rapids, Michigan: William B. Eerdmans Publishing, 1962), 45, 58-59; idem, *A Second Birthday*, 21; idem, *Free in Obedience* (New York: Seabury Press, 1964), 16-17.

4 William Stringfellow, *My People Is the Enemy* (New York: Holt, Rinehard and Winston, 1964), 4-6.

5 Robert Coles, *Dorothy Day: A Radical Devotion* (Reading, Massachusetts: Addison-Wesley Publishing, 1987), 155-56; Stringfellow, *A Second Birthday*, 21.

6 H. G. Little, Jr., review of *Dissenter in a Great Society*, by William Stringfellow, *Theology Today* 23:4 (January 1967), 561; J. D. Douglas, review of *A Private and Public Faith*, by William

Stringfellow, *Evangelical Quarterly* 37:4 (April-June, 1965), 118; John M. Pratt, review of *Dissenter in a Great Society,* by William Stringfellow, *Union Seminary Quarterly Review* 22:1 (November 1966), 63.

7 Stringfellow, *Dissenter in a Great Society,* vii.

8 Ibid., vii; idem, *My People Is the Enemy,* 2, 47.

9 Stringfellow, *A Private and Public Faith,* 56; idem, *A Second Birthday,* 40, 41-43; idem, *An Ethic for Christians and Other Aliens in a Strange Land* (Waco, Texas: Word Books, 1973), 18, 36, chapter title, "The Empirical Integrity of the Biblical Witness," 41.

10 Carter Heyward, "Theologian, Advocate, Friend," *Sojourners* 14:11 (December 1985), 4-5. See also William Stringfellow, *The Life of Worship and the Legal Profession* (Division of College Work of the Episcopal Church, 1955) in which he does not use the word "death" and says nothing of the principalities; idem, "Living Biblically," *Journal of Religious Thought* 37:2 (Fall-Winter 1980-81), 59-60; idem, "Harlem, Rebellion, and Resurrection," 1346; idem, *Free in Obedience,* 24, 26, 50-51.

11 Stringfellow, *Free in Obedience,* 71; idem, *My People Is the Enemy,* 101; idem, "A Lamentation for Easter," *The Witness* 64:4 (April 1981), 5; idem, *A Second Birthday,* 138; idem, *A Private and Public Faith,* 58.

12 William Stringfellow, *Conscience and Obedience: The Politics of Romans 13 and Revelation 13 in Light of the Second Coming* (Waco, Texas: Word Books, 1977), 110.

13 Stringfellow, *A Second Birthday,* 41; idem, *Count It All Joy,* 61; idem, *A Private and Public Faith,* 42, 61; idem, *An Ethic for Christians and Other Aliens in a Strange Land,* 41, 43; idem, *Free in Obedience,* 16, 71; William Stringfellow and Anthony Towne, *Suspect Tenderness: The Ethics of the Berrigan Witness* (New York: Holt, Rinehart and Winston, 1971), 73; Stringfellow, *Conscience and Obedience,* 79, 112.

14 Stringfellow, *An Ethic for Christians and Other Aliens in a Strange Land,* 41; idem, *Free in Obedience,* 70; idem, *Conscience*

and Obedience, 79; idem, "The Politics of Advent," *The Witness* (December 1975), 10, 12.

15 Stringfellow, *An Ethic for Christians and Other Aliens in a Strange Land,* 48; idem, *A Simplicity of Faith,* 134; idem, *Dissenter in a Great Society,* 153; idem, *Suspect Tenderness,* 88-89.

16 *Sojourners* 14:11 (December 1985), especially articles by Jim Wallis, Melvin Schoonover, Jim Forest, and Mary Donnelly; Daniel Berrigan, *To Dwell in Peace; An Autobiography* (San Francisco: Harper, 1987), 254; Thomas Merton, *The Nonviolent Alternative* (New York: Farrar Straus & Giroux, 1980), 259-60; and William Shannon, ed., *The Hidden Ground of Love* (New York: Farrar Straus & Giroux, 1985), 85-86; Thomas Merton, *The Wisdom of the Desert,* 3, 8, 17, 23. Stringfellow and Merton corresponded after Merton read *My People Is the Enemy* (*A Second Birthday,* 191). Stringfellow dedicated *An Ethic for Christians and Other Aliens in a Strange Land* to Merton (in memoriam). Unlike a seminary, which Stringfellow considered insulated from reality, Eschaton was for him as the monastery was for Merton, a way to enter more deeply into reality. Stringfellow's early writings refer to fallen creation and time itself as the Fall (*Conscience and Obedience,* 31, 83).

17 Stringfellow, "Harlem, Rebellion, and Resurrection," 1346, 1348; Helen Waddell, *The Desert Fathers* (Ann Arbor, 1957), 90; Stringfellow, *An Ethic for Christians and Other Aliens in a Strange Land,* 44.

18 Stringfellow, *A Second Birthday,* 99.

19 Stringfellow, *Free in Obedience,* 39; idem, *Instead of Death* (New York: Seabury Press, 1963), 10-12; idem, *Count It All Joy,* 51; idem, *The Politics of Spirituality* (Louisville, Kentucky: Westminster Press, 1984), 20, 38; idem, "The Crisis Accepted," Peter C. Moore, ed., *Youth in Crisis* (New York, 1966), 36; Stringfellow, "Harlem, Rebellion, and Resurrection," 1348.

20 William Apel, "The Dimensions of Death in the Theology of William Stringfellow," *Foundations* 22:4 (October-December 1979), 374; Stringfellow, *A Simplicity of Faith,* 115.

21 Stringfellow, *Suspect Tenderness,* 67-68; idem, *Conscience and Obedience,* 34, 64-65; idem, "A Lamentation for Easter," 6; idem, *An Ethic for Christians and Other Aliens in a Strange Land,* 80, 82; idem, *Free in Obedience,* 31-32; idem, *The Politics of Spirituality,* 66.

22 For his most systematic treatment of the principalities and powers, see Stringfellow, *Free in Obedience,* 52-59.

23 R. Scott Kennedy, "A Step Off America: Life at Eschaton," *Sojourners* 14:11 (December 1985), 20-21; Stringfellow, *Free in Obedience,* 26, 31-32; idem, *A Second Birthday,* 19; idem, *An Ethic for Christians and Other Aliens in a Strange Land,* 48.

24 Stringfellow, *An Ethic for Christians and Other Aliens in a Strange Land,* 154. See also idem, *Dissenter in a Great Society,* end of book; idem, *The Politics of Spirituality,* 62.

25 Stringfellow, *Dissenter in a Great Society,* 26, 29, 33, 40, 100; idem, *A Second Birthday,* 60; *Conscience and Obedience,* 61; idem, *An Ethic for Christians and Other Aliens in a Strange Land,* 154; idem, "Trickle-Down Violence," *Christianity and Crisis* 41:7 (April 27, 1981), 126.

26 Stringfellow, *A Simplicity of Faith,* 76; idem, *The Politics of Spirituality,* 69.

27 Bill Wylie-Kellermann, ed., *A Keeper of the Word: Selected Writings of William Stringfellow* (Grand Rapids, Michigan: William B. Eerdmans Publishing, 1994), 275-79; Stringfellow, *Conscience and Obedience,* 98; idem, "High Crimes and Misdemeanors: The Macabre Era of Kissinger and Nixon," *Sojourners* 13:1 (January 1984), 33; idem, *Suspect Tenderness,* 84; idem, "Why is Novak So Uptight?" *Christianity and Crisis* 30:19 (Nov. 30, 1970), 259; idem, "The Demonic in American Society," *Christianity and Crisis* 29:16 (Sept. 29, 1969), 247; idem, *An Ethic for Christians and Other Aliens in a Strange Land,* 89, 99, 142.

28 William Stringfellow, "Does America Need a Barmen Declaration?" *Christianity and Crisis* 33:22 (Dec. 24, 1973), 274-76; idem, *An Ethic for Christians and Other Aliens in a Strange Land,* 33, 48, 51; idem, *Conscience and Obedience,* 80.

29 Stringfellow, *Free in Obedience,* 92; idem, *Suspect Tenderness,* 67; idem, *A Second Birthday,* 133; idem, *An Ethic for Christians and Other Aliens in a Strange Land,* 17, 110.

30 Edward Long, review of *An Ethic for Christians and Other Aliens in a Strange Land,* by William Stringfellow, *Interpretation* 30:1 (January 1976), 108; Stringfellow, *An Ethic for Christians and Other Aliens in a Strange Land,* 155; idem, *The Politics of Spirituality,* 62, 65; idem, "A Matter of Repentance," *Christianity and Crisis* 39:21 (Jan. 21, 1980), 342; idem, *Free in Obedience,* 92.

31 For a list of his early ecumenical activities, see Stringfellow, *A Second Birthday,* 82-83. Regarding the church's two missions, see idem, *Instead of Death,* 56; idem, *Free in Obedience,* 91-93; idem, *Dissenter in a Great Society,* 143-44; idem, *Count It All Joy,* 35-36.

32 Stringfellow, *A Private and Public Faith,* 41, 75; idem, *Free in Obedience,* 17, 103; idem, *Conscience and Obedience,* 94; idem, *Dissenter in a Great Society,* 69, 142; idem, *My People Is the Enemy,* 40.

33 Stringfellow, *Free in Obedience,* 20, 26, 38, 82; idem, "The Witness of a Remnant," *The Witness* 72:11 (November 1989) [reprint of 1979 address to the Episcopal Peace Fellowship], 23; idem, *My People Is the Enemy,* 135; William Stringfellow and Anthony Towne, *The Death and Life of Bishop Pike* (Garden City, New York: Doubleday, 1976). See also William Stringfellow, "The State of the Church," *The Witness* 62:5 (May 1979), 4; idem, *A Private and Public Faith,* 23; idem, "The Church in Exile," *The Witness* 58:8 (March 9, 1975), 6.

34 Concerning Constantine, see especially William Stringfellow, "Justification, the Consumption Ethic, and Vocational Poverty," *Christianity and Crisis* 36:6 (April 12, 1976), 78; idem, *Conscience and Obedience,* 48-51; idem, "On Being Haunted by the Angel of the Church at Sardis," *The Witness* 58 (September 1975), 4-5; idem, "The Politics of Pastoral Care: An Ecumenical Meditation Concerning the Incumbent Pope," *The Witness* 67:2 (February 1984), 13. The reference to John the Baptist and Herod is drawn from Ignazio Silone's 1936 novel, *Bread and Wine* (New York: Signet Classic, 1986), 217-18.

35 Stringfellow, *A Private and Public Faith*, 11; idem, *Free in Obedience*, 95; idem, *An Ethic for Christians and Other Aliens in a Strange Land*, 121.

36 Stringfellow, *Conscience and Obedience*, 104; idem, *An Ethic for Christians and Other Aliens in a Strange Land*, 59-60; idem, foreward to Melvin Schoonover, *Making All Things Human: A Church in East Harlem* (New York, 1969), viii; Stringfellow, *A Second Birthday*, 153-54; idem, *Suspect Tenderness*, 113.

37 For his fullest discussions of the circus, see Stringfellow, *A Second Birthday*, 167-70; idem, *A Simplicity of Faith*, 87-91. Stringfellow romanticized the circus, ignoring its negative sides—the abuse of "freaks," the mistreatment of animals, the shadow side of clowning—with a charity he never allowed the church. See also idem, *A Simplicity of Faith*, 55; idem, *A Second Birthday*, 168.

38 Stringfellow, *Conscience and Obedience*, 14, 25, 102; idem, "A Lamentation for Easter," 6; idem, *Dissenter in a Great Society*, 126-27 160; idem, *The Politics of Spirituality*, 61; idem, *Suspect Tenderness*, 102. The anti-Nazi Resistance movement seemed to bequeath some of Dietrich Bonhoeffer's ethics to Stringfellow through a brief contact in 1947 (Stringfellow, *An Ethic for Christians and Other Aliens in a Strange Land*, 117-18). Two titles of Stringfellow's books introduce the theme: *Free in Obedience* and *Conscience and Obedience*.

39 Stringfellow, *An Ethic for Christians and Other Aliens in a Strange Land*, 138-39.

40 Ibid., 63-64, 118-20, 151-53; Thomas Merton, "A Letter to Pablo Antonio Cuadra Concerning Giants," *The Collected Poems of Thomas Merton* (New York: New Directions, 1977), 391; Stringfellow, *Dissenter in a Great Society*, 10-11.

41 Stringfellow, *A Second Birthday*, 196-97.

42 William Stemper, review of *An Ethic for Christians and Other Aliens in a Strange Land*, by William Stringfellow, *Union Seminary Quarterly Review* 31:2 (Winter 1976), 148; Ralph Heynan, review of *A Second Birthday*, by William Stringfellow, *Calvin Theological*

Journal 6:1 (April 1971), 73; editor's preface to "Harlem, Rebellion, and Resurrection," *The Christian Century* 87:45 (Nov. 11, 1970), 1338; Stringfellow, *A Second Birthday*, 145-46; Bruce Kenrick, *Come Out the Wilderness: The Story of East Harlem Protestant Parish* (New York: Harper and Row, 1962), 143.

43 Stringfellow, *The Politics of Spirituality*, 53; idem, *An Ethic for Christians and Other Aliens in a Strange Land*, 14; idem *My People Is the Enemy*, 27-28; idem, "An Open Letter to the Presiding Bishop," *The Witness* 63:1 (January 1980), 11; idem, "Witness of a Remnant," 21; idem, "The State of the Church," 4.

44 William Stringfellow and Anthony Towne, *The Bishop Pike Affair: Scandals of Conscience and Heresy, Relevance and Solemnity in the Contemporary Church* (New York, Harper and Row, 1967), especially 94-114.

45 Stringfellow, *A Private and Public Faith*, 22; idem, *Dissenter in a Great Society*, 162; idem, *Free in Obedience*, 44; idem, "The Bible and Ideology," *Sojourners* 5:7 (September 1976), 7; idem, "The Politics of Pastoral Care," 14.

46 Stringfellow, *Dissenter in a Great Society*, 132; Russell Hutchinson, review of *An Ethic for Christians and Other Aliens in a Strange Land*, by William Stringfellow, *Religious Education* 69:3 (May-June 1974), 396; Stringfellow, *A Simplicity of Faith*, 116, 132-33.

47 James Holloway, "It Was an Adventure," *Sojourners* 14:11 (December 1985), 27; Stringfellow, *An Ethic for Christians and Other Aliens in a Strange Land*, 21; Joseph Bettis, review of *An Ethic for Christians and Other Aliens in a Strange Land*, by William Stringfellow, *Journal of the American Academy of Religion* 43:2 (June 1975), 393-94; William Stringfellow, "Election Reflections," *Christianity and Crisis* 32:20 (Nov. 27, 1972), 258; idem, *A Simplicity of Faith*, 141. The kinship between Stringfellow and John of Patmos is noted by Dennis MacDonald, "John on the Island of Patmos and William on the Island of Block," *Post-American* 3:7 (October 1974), 18-19.

48 Stringfellow, *The Politics of Spirituality,* 39, 45.

49 R. Scott Kennedy, "A Step Off America," 20; Stringfellow, *An Ethic for Christians and Other Aliens in a Strange Land,* 16. William Wendt, "To Mourn and Celebrate," *Sojourners* 14:11 (December 1985), 28, called the book of Revelation "the seed bed for [Stringfellow's] life and thought." Stringfellow's passion for Revelation is another clue to the similarity between his own vocation and that of John of Patmos.

THE DIALECTICS OF FAITH

TIMOTHY F. SEDGWICK

There are two cities in which we live: the city of mortals and the city of God. The one is a temporal, earthly city. The other is an eternal, heavenly city. One seeks to secure all that perishes. The other gives thanks for all that is, in dying. One is a city of death, the other a city of life. One is a city at war with itself, the other a city at peace. In the one all are slaves; in the other there is freedom. The city of mortals has many names. Biblically that city is called Babylon, but it is just as accurately called Rome, New York, Paris, Berlin, Washington, Beijing, or Buenos Aires. The city of God is, however, singular. Though beyond time, this city is just as surely known: it is the basis for knowing that we live in cities which are fallen.

Our knowledge of the city of God is not some kind of knowledge about the world, like whether or not it will be sunny or rainy tomorrow. Our knowledge of this city is a personal kind of knowledge, given in our relationship one to another. Such knowledge is an acknowledgment of the indubitable truth we experience one to another, as when we know that we are known, accepted, and loved. Such knowledge is saving knowledge, knowledge that we live in a divine city that makes us whole, even now as we live amidst the city of mortals.

As Christians, the truth of our life is revealed in Jesus Christ, now in Word and sacrament. As William Stringfellow wrote in his first book in 1962, *A Private and Public Faith*, "when, now and then, I turn to and listen to the Bible, or when, now and then, I hear the Word of God exposed in preaching, or when, now and then, I see the gospel represented in the Holy Communion . . . I thereupon become a participant in and witness of the real life which is given to the world."[1] In his own life, he gave expression to this life. That is to say, he gave expression to Christian faith as that which arose from two poles, from his life as a Christian and from his life as a lawyer, social activist, public lecturer, member of the Episcopal Church, political and social critic. Church and world, Christ and culture, faith and daily life were not two separate realities but, instead, two poles which together drew him out of himself and into a newness of life which death could not overcome.

Stringfellow wrote in order to make sense out of his life, not narrowly as an individual but as a human person connected to the rest of the world. In this sense, he was an autobiographical thinker. He could only make sense out of his life in light of the Word of God, in interpreting and responding to his actual situation in life as given by God in light of the Christian story as given and celebrated in scripture and in worship. "*We* are each one of us parables," says Stringfellow.[2] And so, in the details of our lives, God's presence is shockingly, surprisingly revealed. But more than a confessional writer, Stringfellow was an evangelist. He shared what he had been given because that was the nature of the gospel.

Stringfellow's own life offers a proclamation of the gospel: East Harlem resident and poverty lawyer; political dissident; protester in civil disobedience, indicted for harboring a fugitive, the Jesuit Daniel Berrigan who had protested the War in Vietnam by pouring blood on draft files; church lawyer supporting Bishop James Pike against accusations of heresy; social critic and orator. All of this was done in the midst of life-threatening illness, recovery, and continued bodily frailty lived in the simplicity of a home on Block Island off of Rhode Island with poet Anthony Towne. It was fed by reading of the Bible and table fellowship, connected to the world and drawn out in the world by friendships and a sense of call to celebrate and share the life given to him in faith. The sheer power of these events gives voice to Christian faith incarnate in the world. The story of Stringfellow, however, tends too easily to overshadow his constructive contribution to understanding Christian faith and to doing theology.

Such omission is particularly regrettable, because Stringfellow is the most significant dialectical theologian in the United States since Reinhold Niebuhr. Like Niebuhr, Stringfellow demonstrates that at the heart of Christian faith is a reconciliation which is not individualistic but corporate, to be drawn out and connected to all people and all of creation. This corporate understanding of faith is itself grounded in the experience of such grace in the everyday life of the world as that is given and revealed in scripture and worship, in Word and sacrament. The Christian life is then a matter of acknowledgment and response, what Stringfellow calls an ethic of witness. This gives the greatest clarity to the nature of the Church and its mission and to the vocation of the Christian. In a word, Stringfellow offers a truly evangelical theology that is sacramental rather than pietistic, social rather than individualistic, incarnational rather than otherworldly.

Dialectical theology may be contrasted with philosophical theologies in which faith is understood in terms of human experience and understanding.[3] Philosophical theologies are, in this sense, based on analogical reasoning: what we say about God is a matter of moving from human experience and understanding of the world to attribute like qualities to God. Scripture itself makes such moves. The Israelites experienced God in the face of the stranger and in an embrace of those in need which, in turn, gave freedom from bondage and hope for the future. As told in the experience of the Exodus, and proclaimed anew in the prophets, God is redeemer and liberator who cares for the poor. What exactly such redemption means in history is itself the story of scripture, a story of declaration and exploration, judgment and change, in both experience and understanding. By way of analogy, philosophical theologies see in Jesus that God is not the warrior God of the nation, and that suffering is of the essence of things, that God is then a God of suffering and that redemption happens in the midst of suffering.

Philosophical theologies seek to make sense of Christian faith and, thereby, to deepen the faith that is in us. They are, as Anselm said, a matter of faith seeking understanding. Clement of Alexandria, Origen, Augustine, Anselm, Thomas Aquinas, Richard Hooker,

Friedrich Schleiermacher—such theologians have given philosophical expression to Christian faith, developed systematically in terms of doctrine, of what can be rightfully said about God, Christ, and God's ongoing work in the world. So, for example, to say God is love is to say that the human experience of love participates in the ultimate ground and purpose of life itself. What is the nature of such love is then the subject of exploration: love as pleasure, love as fulfillment, love as service, love as friendship, love as sacrifice. As the name implies, the problem of philosophical theologies is that they can become philosophies, theories of knowledge abstracted from the daily experience from which the analogies themselves are drawn. God can become an object in itself, separate from human life. Faith itself can become narrowed to belief.

The first of the Christian dialectical thinkers is the apostle Paul. Paul found himself founded anew in Christ, on the other side of what was experienced as a great chasm. As described in his Letter to the Romans, Paul looks back upon his former life as a Jew as a life lived under the law, as seeking righteousness or wholeness by living in accord with the law. He describes this as a life of works righteousness, a life he now sees as futile, leading only to despair. What the law does is detail what we should do in order to be fulfilled. In the demand we feel our impotence and, more, our bondage. We cannot do what we want to do (Romans 7:15). The more we try, the more we experience judgment in the absence of any real connectedness to what we more deeply desire. "The end is death" (Romans 6:21). But through Christ, Paul stands on the other side. Now he experiences the presence of God, not as something to be achieved but as a presence in life regardless, as a matter of grace. One is justified by grace (Romans 3:24, 28). In contrast to death, one now lives in eternal life, life that is spoken of as eternal in the sense that it cannot be taken away (Romans 6:23). "Nothing can separate us from the love of God" (Romans 8:23). We then "do not live to ourselves, and we do not die to ourselves . . . . we live to the Lord, and if we die, we die to the Lord; so then, whether we live or whether we die, we are the Lord's" (Romans 14:7). Such a life is then marked by a spontaneous love and a new freedom to care for one another.

Paul is dialectic in that the meaning of faith is given in the juxta-position of the new with the old. The change is so radical that it is impossible to describe Christian faith and life in terms of the old, except as its opposite. Law and grace, flesh and spirit, death and life, Adam and Christ: the meaning of faith is itself given in these con-trasts. Analogical reasoning is, from this point of view, misguided at best. To find a point of contact between common human experience and the experience of God is to lose the radical conversion which is at the heart of Christian faith. At worst, any such attempt at philo-sophical theology is idolatrous in once again making God into an end or experience to be achieved instead of a reality that simply is, that acts upon us, that transforms our lives, and is the basis for our very being. Faith can only be spoken from within the circle of faith as the story of God in Christ. In typically dialectical fashion, Martin Luther said, as Pauline Protestant reformer, "Aristotle is the antichrist."

Dialectical theologies have arisen consistently alongside of philo-sophical theologies, especially among those who experience the dis-junctions of life, the contradictions and absurdities. Mystics are, for example, dialectical in their thought, as when Meister Eckhardt opposes God to the God about which we speak. In this opposition between God and the God above God, we are brought to silence and the experience of both the sheer transcendence and presence of God. Probably the most consistently and ruthlessly dialectical theologian was Søren Kierkegaard. Kierkegaard's influence on contemporary theology cannot be overstated. His dialectical thought arose in oppo-sition to the philosophy of Hegel, who sought to describe God in terms of the developing spirit or purpose of the world. No thought could be more philosophical than Hegel's in the sense that philoso-phy was the articulation of the idea of God in history. For Kierkegaard, however, this reduced God to an ethical ideal, the great-est good as the end of history. Given evil and human suffering, he could not imagine such an achievement. Even more, to make God the end was to make God contingent on, dependent on humanity. This form of works righteousness made impossible the actual experience of God and hence salvation. Faith could only rest on the pure experi-ence of God apart from the end. Then, and only then, in faith is the moral funded, not as demand but as the expression of something given that is more fundamental.

Kierkegaard's dialectical thought is nowhere more powerful than in his stories. For example, in his retelling of the story of Abraham and the sacrifice of Isaac in *Fear and Trembling*, Abraham holds simultaneously to the contradictory claims that God has promised a future through his first-born son Isaac and that God has demanded the sacrifice of Isaac, that the law must be obeyed and that God had demanded the abrogation of the law, that God will take Isaac in sacrifice and that God will provide. There is no resolution here between the ethical and the religious. Instead, Kierkegaard describes the human experience of faith and morals as they arise in full conflict and contradiction, neither to be lost or resolved in the other. In the dialectic is the experience of God. In the dialectic, faith is born.

As Kierkegaard was the dialectical theologians' answer to the philosophical theology of Hegel, Karl Barth—and what came to be called neo-orthodoxy—was the dialectical answer to the philosophical theology of liberalism. While liberal theology sought to make sense of Christian faith in light of the modern world, Barth turned such thought on its head: he sought to make sense of the world in terms of the Christian faith as given in the Bible and specifically in the story of God and our salvation as revealed in Jesus Christ. In this dialectical thought, the Bible is no fundamentalistic, literal text that describes the world—as if it were a book of biology and ethics, physics and metaphysics, history and after-history. Instead, the Bible creates as it construes the world. Personal language alone is adequate to the experience of scripture and the coming to religious faith. Scripture is the Word of God. In and through scripture, God addresses the listeners, judges them, declares them whole, and invites them into a new world and a new relationship with God.

William Stringfellow stands clearly in this tradition of dialectical theology. What is distinctive is that the dialectics of faith are developed in terms of social, political metaphors: Babylon and Jerusalem, the city of death and the city of God, sovereign and slave. Central to these poles is the sense that the newness and fullness of life come only in becoming a people, connected to all of humanity and finally to creation itself. Only as a people are we reconciled, connected beyond ourselves, beyond an individualism in which death is the final word. The Pauline dialectic of justification by works and justification by grace through faith has too often become narrowly focused on the individual and his or her salvation. This is reflected in the very shortening of the phrase "justification by grace through faith" to "justification by faith." The emphasis thereby shifts from the larger work of God in reconciling all of creation to a focus on the individual's experience of reconciliation.

This individualistic focus was particularly given by Martin Luther as he sought reconciliation within the rigorism of the monastic life. More scrupulous confession of sins and devoted prayers of penance only drove Luther further into despair. The reading of Paul was for Luther the hearing of the Word of God. Through the work of Christ, God has forgiven all who sin. Salvation is not a matter of works but of grace. And while this meant the completion of God's work begun in Abraham to form a people, the focus on the experience of justification by grace through Christ came to focus on faith as an act of acceptance of beliefs about Jesus Christ. Stringfellow himself describes such a view as pietistic and fundamentalistic, reflecting most especially the individualism of American religion given its privatization of religion from matters of the state.

The greatest expression in American theology of this larger sense of reconciliation as a matter of becoming a people—at least until the development of liberation thought—was given by Reinhold Niebuhr. Salvation was for Niebuhr always communal. The dialectics of human life in response to God were then developed in terms of what he called the dialectical relationship between love and justice. "The achievements of justice in history may rise in indeterminate degrees to find their fulfillment in a more perfect love and brotherhood; but each new level of fulfillment also contains elements which stand in contradiction to perfect love . . . . The love commandment is therefore no simple historical possibility . . . [but] illustrates the dialectical relation between history and the eternal." In this dialectic is grace itself given.[4] This is Reinhold Niebuhr at his best. At other times, however, Niebuhr's moral vocabulary—of which love and justice are central—

focuses reconciliation not on the experience of grace as that is given corporately but, instead, focuses reconciliation on the end as an ideal, what he called in his earlier writing "the impossible possibility."[5]

Stringfellow himself grounds the larger corporate understanding of Christian faith in the experience of God. "I know nothing about God," says Stringfellow, "in a speculative or hypothetical sense, and I am able to speak of Him only out of my own experience of His presence, on the one hand, in the common life of the world as I participate in it, and, on the other hand, the life of the Church as I participate in that."[6] This experience of God begins in the experience of crisis, in the inability to sustain any sense of meaning that would be enduring. This "*[u]tter* helplessness . . . is an experience in which all is given up, in which all effort and activity of whatever sort ceases, not only in which all answers are unknown, but unattempted, and also in which all questions are inarticulated and abandoned."[7] This is "the primitive experience of faith" of "dying to the preposterous arrogance of trying to save one's self." This is the experience of "the claim of death over all of life," that "all" to which humans "attach significance for their existence"[8] are but idols—family, nation, culture, pleasure, money, honor, fame, beliefs, religion and the Church, as well as death, demanding as it does the absolute, endless, and all-consuming attempt to conquer death.

The cross is the ultimate and complete revelation of faith. "The crucifixion," says Stringfellow, "is pre-eminently the event which brings all of the ordinary issues of existence in this world within the province of the gospel."[9] Jesus' death brings together the renunciation of all idols, including death itself, with the corresponding experience of utter helplessness. "My God, my God, why have you forsaken me?" "Into your hands, O Lord, I commend my spirit." In this offering of the self is the experience of God given. This again is best expressed in personal terms. The experience of grace is the experience of cross and resurrection as revealed in Jesus Christ. God acts upon us. Life is a gift, and you are inextricably part of this life regardless of what you do or what happens to you. Stringfellow expresses this most personally in his book, *A Second Birthday*.

Stringfellow's health had continued to decline after he and Anthony Towne moved in 1967 to Block Island. This reached a climax in the spring of 1968, when he lost sixty pounds in seven weeks. Pancreatitis and the consequent inability to digest and absorb food, combined with an increasing, focused pain, brought Stringfellow and his friends to the conclusion that he would soon die. A final operation found a growth on the pancreas and a nearly ruptured spleen. Both organs were removed. Miraculously, Stringfellow survived the six-hour operation. More miraculously, Stringfellow lived. Spiritually, in this movement into death, he died to death itself and was resurrected. In commending himself to God in utter helplessness, Stringfellow experienced the full power of God as grace. He concludes *A Second Birthday*, "life is a gift which death does not vitiate or void: faith is the acceptance, honoring, rejoicing in that gift. That being so, in my own story, *it did not matter whether I died.* Read no resignation or indifference into this confession. It is freedom from moral bondage to death that enables a man to live humanly and to die at any moment without concern."[10]

In more theological language, Stringfellow expresses the experience of God as a matter of providence and resurrection. "[P]rovidence means the constant and continual renewal of God's grace in all situations for every man throughout time . . . . no circumstances ever arise which are beyond God's care or reach . . . . the power and reality of death at work concretely in the world is never so ascendant or successful that resurrection—the transcendence of death and the restoration of life—is either irrelevant or precluded."[11] Always, the experience of God's absolute grace for Stringfellow is given in life itself. "That Jesus Christ descends into Hell means that as we die (in any sense of the term *die*) our expectation in death is encounter with the Word of God, which is, so to speak, already there in the midst of death."[12]

The absolute experience of grace is itself inseparable from its meaning. As a Christian, this means grace is inseparable from Jesus Christ. Stringfellow then refers to the experience of God as the experience of grace as two-sided, as having a double reference: first, to the experience itself, and, second, to that which uncovers and makes manifest this experience. He calls this double-sided experience "the Word of God" rather than simply grace or the experience of God in order to convey the inseparability of the two references. The Word of

God refers both to the sign and to the event. "Though the Word of God," says Stringfellow, "dwells in the world and is present within the common life of the world, not every person by any means knows or acknowledges that presence in history and in his own action and experience."[13] This comes only in confronting and surrendering all attempts to control and overcome "the presence and power of death." But, concludes Stringfellow, no one "confronts and struggles with and surrenders to any of the powers of death—any anxieties—any crisis—without beholding the power and the truth of the Resurrection: the presence of God in history which is greater than any of death's threats or temptations—and more potent—and which endures forever."[14] The Word of God is not, then, any more identical with scripture itself than with the experience of grace in itself. Rather, scripture is the Word of God as it interprets us and brings us into the presence of God. The Word of God indicates the event of grace and reconciliation effected as scripture uncovers and makes manifest the experience of God.

Worship is likewise the Word of God for Stringfellow. In worship—and especially Holy Communion or Eucharist—Jesus' life, taken up into God in his death on the cross, is celebrated and enacted. In this way worship uncovers and makes manifest the experience of God. Such worship is called sacramental in the sense that by sacrament is meant that which uncovers and manifests, reveals and makes present. This is in fact how sacraments have been defined in the Christian tradition. They are actions which "effect by signifying."[15] As revealed in Eucharist, what is at the heart of this event of grace is the offering up of the self to God and in that offering the experience of grace and connectedness to all that is.

> Christian worship that has integrity is never a particular offering of possessions, conduct or other tribute considered pleasing and acceptable to God; it is always the offering of all that one is, that which seems good or of which one is proud as well as that which does not seem good or of which one is ashamed. Christians offer themselves, their whole selves . . . knowing that no one and nothing so offered in worship is acceptable to God in and of itself. Yet this unacceptable offering is rendered worthy by God's acceptance of it. The Christian offering, far from resembling religious

sacrifices, is the offering of one's self as a sinner and as a representative of all others as sinners in confidence in the mercy of God's sufficient sacrifice for all.[16]

Eucharist is at the center of Christian worship. In Eucharist, Christians stand together under the sign of God's judgment and promise in Christ that all are reconciled as they share in these events of death and resurrection, in the breaking of bread and drinking of wine as these are the body and blood of Christ.

In this account of Christian faith, Stringfellow has offered a dialectic of faith that is corporate. Again, in Protestant thought the dialectic of law and gospel—justification by works and justification by grace—focuses attention on the individual in relationship to God. The primary model in these metaphors is, after all, judicial: the individual stands before God to be judged. Sacrifice is accordingly understood in terms of Jesus taking on the punishment meant for humanity, thereby meeting the demands of justice so that all might enter into relationship with God.[17] In contrast, for Stringfellow the primary dialectic of faith is existential, but an understanding of existence that is social and political: death and grace are given in the dialectic of Babylon and Jerusalem, the city of death and the city of God, sovereign and slave.

Justification for Stringfellow gains its meaning not from a judicial meaning of unrighteousness but from the political meaning of injustice. There is no human justice, societies in which all relations are right, whole, complete. Claims of being just—for example, America as a just and holy nation—are all forms of idolatry. Justification arises, then, in the loss and negation of these idols. When they come to naught and are seen as expressions of the larger rule of death, then we become utterly helpless and available to the grace of God. Then there is justification, "a sustained experience of being whole and holy" in which a person is in right relation with all of creation.[18]

Stringfellow's corporate understanding of reconciliation and redemption is given in his experience of the Word of God as his experience of faith is uncovered and manifest in scripture and worship. Paul's sense of justification is primary for Stringfellow. He once had a class of older youth from East Harlem simply read Paul's Letter to the Romans, because in that reading, and listening, he knew the Word of God was to be heard.[19] But Paul is read in the larger social and political context of the Church and society reflected especially in the pastoral epistles. Many of Stringfellow's central writings take these as the point of departure: *Free in Obedience* (1964) is a commentary on the Letter to the Hebrews; *Count It All Joy* (1967) arises from a reading of the Letter to James; *An Ethic for Christians and Other Aliens in a Strange Land* (1973)[20] finds the Word of God in the Book of Revelation; *Conscience and Obedience* (1977) moves between the Letter to the Romans and the Book of Revelation.[21]

The Eucharist as the other center of the Word of God further insures a corporate understanding of reconciliation and redemption. The gathering of the community of faith in "the congregation's sacramental life in worship," says Stringfellow, "is not only an event of remembrance and preview: the Church is as well engaged in celebrating the reconciliation known now and already within the Church on behalf of the world."[22] As a gathering of the community, as table fellowship, as formed in faith together in the offering of themselves in praise and thanksgiving for the gift of life that has been given, reconciliation and redemption are corporate. Communion is "the new community in Christ,"[23] itself a witness and sacrament of God's grace and rule.

Throughout his account of worship, Stringfellow sustains his dialectical thought so that neither a particular experience nor a particular rendering of that experience is identified with God's grace and rule. The Church as a sacrament, as the Word of God, is always in danger of confusing its particular form of worship, beliefs, or fellowship with God. Stringfellow counters such identification in identifying the revelation of God in worship itself, in the offering of oneself to God in repentance, in intercession for the world, and in thanksgiving. More, worship as offering can itself become confused so that the act of worship becomes identified with the experience of God apart from the entirety of life in the world. However, Stringfellow is clear: such worship would be no offering of the whole of the human self, "of our selves, our souls and bodies" (as the prayer just before Holy

Communion commended the worshiper in the *Book of Common Prayer* which Stringfellow used in worship). Worship would itself then become the object of faith rather than a witness to God in which the self is drawn outside of itself, reconciled to God and all of creation.

The dialectic between worship and life in the world, between Church and world, is thus established. Each requires the other as each informs and effects the other. "[W]orship in the congregation and witness in the world must be integral to one another. There is no solitary witness of a Christian in the world, isolated from the congregation, because the sacramental worship in the congregation is the comprehensive and exemplary Christian witness in the world . . . . the Christian bears the tension between the gospel and the world in radical and transforming witness only because he participates in the event of the congregation."[24] The fullness of the gospel is witnessed as the eucharistic celebration and offering of life is informed and realized by the Christian life in the world. "The sacramental events in the congregation exemplify the witness of Christians in the world; the witness in the world gives content to the forms of sacramental life in the congregation. Each authorizes and authenticates the other."[25]

Stringfellow's sacramental and incarnational understanding is then expressed in his understanding of Christian vocation as fundamentally that of witness. "The daily witness of the Christian in the world," he says, "is essentially sacramental, rather than moralistic. . . . The ethics of witness to redemption are sacramental ethics of grace, rather than of prudence or of law."[26]Any attempt to identify the Christian life with a particular set of judgments—even the pacifist renunciation of violence[27]—is to step outside the dialectics of faith. Any such attempt is, in the end, an attempt to secure identity in a set of actions or way of life. In contrast, the center and source of Christian faith is in the acknowledgment of God: "the adoration of the Creator, the praise and gratitude of creation for the generosity of God, the celebration of life as a gift, or, simply, the worship of God."[28] Moral judgments may and must be made, but they are not to be confused with Christian faith. What is rather the first and last word is "the freedom to live now, for all the strife and ambiguity and travail, in the imminent transcendence of death, and all of death's threats and temptations. That is the gift of

God to men and women in Christ's Resurrection."[29]

The enduring significance of Stringfellow is not as Christian philosophical theologian and ethicist. His writings rather provide a dialectical proclamation of the Word of God by moving back and forth between a reading of scripture and worship and a reading of the world in which he found himself. This reading of faith and culture, however, provides such a powerful cultural critique and witness to Christian faith—personalized and amplified by Stringfellow's own life—that it easily overshadows the constructive foundations of Stringfellow's thought. In developing the dialectics of faith in corporate terms, grounded in a sacramental and incarnational understanding of the world, Stringfellow offers a broader and more adequate account of the dialectics of faith than has been generally provided in the dialectical tradition of theology. Such a corporate, sacramental, and incarnational vision has more often been associated with the more philosophical accounts of faith given by Roman Catholics, Orthodox, and Anglicans. Such a vision certainly reflects the best of the sacramental theologies of these traditions.[30] Less able, however, have these traditions been in providing a dialectical witness to that faith.

NOTES

1 William Stringfellow, *A Private and Public Faith* (Grand Rapids, Michigan: William B. Eerdmans Publishing, 1962), 14.

2 William Stringfellow, *A Simplicity of Faith: My Experience in Mourning* (Nashville: Abingdon Press, 1982), 20.

3 On the different types of theology see Hans Frei, *Types of Christian Theology*, George Hunsinger and William C. Placher, eds. (New Haven: Yale University Press, 1992).

4 Reinhold Niebuhr, *The Nature and Destiny of Man, Vol. II* (New York: Charles Scribner's Sons, 1943), 246. See especially the concluding chapter, "The End of History," 287-321.

5 Reinhold Niebuhr, *An Interpretation of Christian Ethics* (New York:

Harper and Row, 1935). The moral idealism here is the basis for his dialectical reading of politics in terms of ideal and real, for example, *Moral Man and Immoral Society* (New York: Charles Scribner's Sons, 1932).

6 Stringfellow, *A Private and Public Faith*, 58-59.

7 William Stringfellow, *Count It All Joy* (Grand Rapids, Michigan: William B. Eerdmans Publishing, 1967), 47-48.

8 Ibid., 50-52.

9 William Stringfellow, *Free in Obedience* (New York: Seabury Press, 1964), 16.

10 William Stringfellow, *A Second Birthday* (Garden City, New York: Doubleday, 1970), 203.

11 Ibid., 121.

12 Stringfellow, *A Simplicity of Faith*, 110. This is referred to and interpreted in the same way as well in his first book, *A Private and Public Faith*, 63.

13 Stringfellow, *A Private and Public Faith*, 62.

14 Ibid., 64.

15 See Karl Rahner, "Introductory Observations on Thomas Aquinas' Theology of the Sacraments in General," *Theological Investigations* 14 (London: Darton, Longman, and Todd, 1976), 149-60. See also "What Is a Sacrament?", 135-48.

16 Stringfellow, *Count It All Joy*, 33.

17 On classical models see Ed Farley, *Good and Evil* (Minneapolis, Minnesota: Augsburg Fortress, 1990), 124-30.

18 William Stringfellow, "Justice and Justification," *The Politics of Spirituality* (Louisville, Kentucky: Westminster Press, 1984), 47-68.

19 Stringfellow, *Count It All Joy*, 60-72.

20 William Stringfellow, *An Ethic for Christians and Other Aliens in a Strange Land* (Waco, Texas: Word Books, 1973).

21 William Stringfellow, *Conscience and Obedience* (Waco, Texas:

Word Books, 1977).

22 Stringfellow, *Free in Obedience*, 118.

23 Ibid., 123.

24 Ibid., 123-24.

25 Ibid., 125-26.

26 Ibid., 39.

27 Stringfellow, *An Ethic for Christians and Other Aliens in a Strange Land*, 132.

28 Stringfellow, *Conscience and Obedience*, 29.

29 Stringfellow, *Count It All Joy*, 93.

30 For an overview of eucharistic sacramental theology see William R. Crockett, *Eucharist, Symbol of Transformation* (New York: Pueblo Publishing, 1989). On the Anglican tradition see Louis Weil, *Sacraments and Liturgy* (Oxford: M. Basil Blackwell Inc., 1983).

A PROPHET OF THE
BIBLICAL WORLD

WILLIAM R. COATES

I first met William Stringfellow in the spring of 1963. It was at General Theological Seminary in New York. I was at the end of my second year of study to be an Episcopal priest. He had been invited to speak to the student body on the racial crisis. At that point he had something of a public reputation, at least in church circles. His work in Harlem had not gone unnoticed and his first book, *A Private Faith*, was being discussed among those church people slowly emerging from the somnolent fifties into the increasingly charged political air of the early sixties.

He spoke rather woodenly, standing behind a podium in formal style. He was in fact gripping the podium; he had been drinking. There were no notes. He spoke freely, with a low, threatening tone. He wove together a recital of racial woe and biblical commentary. We had never heard anything so direct, piercing, and menacing.

He wore a business suit and sported close-cropped hair, like a career major in his tenth military year. In those early days militancy did not advertise itself in a distinctive dress. Indeed later, when who you were was announced by what you wore, Stringfellow still came packaged the same way. What did the exterior matter anyway?

He spoke in quiet, direct tones. You often had to lean forward to pick up the words. The drama was mostly in the content, but the tone added a subdued ferocity to the event. His speech was sarcastic, pained, searing but never loud or abrasive. At some point as he droned on about the hypocrisy of prejudice and the cruelty of oppression, about complicity and Christian evasion, about the corruption of the church and the need for radical political engagement, we sensed that the whole of our comfortable seminary education, with its complacent adhesion to Anglican pieties, was for naught. As the indictment mounted, the room became restless, the mood ascending toward open resentment.

Here was a prophet! Of course we had all taken our classes in Hebrew prophecy and assumed we knew just what they were saying, but in that room prophecy took on a different meaning for me. I was familiar with the content of Hebrew prophecy: the fierce adherence to social justice. But learning about the prophets and experiencing one in the here-and-now are two different things. Prophecy is not a thing, not a teaching, not simply shocking content. It is an occasion. What is forever lost to us because of the multiple layers of biblical transmissions is the occasion itself. Why did the people hate Jeremiah so and why did they want Jesus killed? As we from our betraying distance read the old biblical words, we can't really catch why murder seemed such a logical conclusion to those enemies of the prophets. Prophetic words make sense and have a logic we find convincing. Something, however, has been distilled. It isn't the prophetic anger (for it isn't clear the prophets ranted much), and beyond the parables their oral pronouncements may not have been theatrical at all. Yet somehow it was the occasion which provoked as much as the words, and the occasion has been lost to us. Here we were, in the present, experiencing a prophetic occasion and responding with disbelief, anger, and resentment. Clearly things hadn't changed much since biblical times.

Listening to Stringfellow that day made me think of prophecy anew. In part, it was Stringfellow's directness, the accusation, the slow, elaborated indictment. There was also his strange sense of emotional distance from his words. Statements and claims were made as if they had a reality of their own, imminent of fulfillment, and were not really a part of or even dependent on the mood, intelligence, or attention of the speaker. They were the Word of God, which in this case meant they had an independent reality and power now swooping onto history's plane. What difference did it make who spoke them or what the speaker's disposition was?

Stringfellow's address was an odd combination of weariness and menace, of flatness and apocalyptic warning. We were being stung by his indictment, drawn into a vast conspiracy of wrong, so common in prophetic address. But how could we, trained to think that America had escaped the history of treachery and monstrous destruction so inbred in Europe and Asia, take in words piercing the American world. Such is the task of prophets. They unveil the cruel contradiction on which all societies rest. They lay bare the lie on which all public life, so zealous to guard power and privilege, is based. Slowly, inexorably, our public life was being unmasked. We became frightened because, if Stringfellow was right, then the edifice of church life and political life was itself mendacious, distorted, and we were caught in a trap from which no amount of church or liberal pieties could extricate us. All prophets are apocalyptic, not in the sense that they deal with doom in a blazing future or have nightmarish visions of an historical outcome hidden from others, but because they understand society and political life to be based on lies (and violence). They cannot tolerate the public fictions which the rest of us not only tolerate but welcome and perpetuate. The prophets display God's woundedness and contempt for the web of mendacity which supports civil society. After the prophets speak there is no place to hide. None of this can be grasped merely by reading the Hebrew prophets. You have to experience the quicksand, which is the occasion. The words of the prophets are not written on the subway walls, they are enunciated in tremulous occasions from which one never recovers. After the occasion, one lives in society as if that society was the harbor of death itself. I don't think I ever recovered from that night. This was the prophetic world of Bill Stringfellow. It was foremost a biblical world.

I remember the end of the talk. We were restless by that time, convicted. Then, he concluded, because of our history, because of racism and the humiliation of black Americans, there would come a time, he said, when black rage would no longer wait for white redress; there would come a time, he said, when a white person would be walking on a city street, and, out from a car or a building a black man armed with a knife would attack. The long history of white oppression would spill out and be visited on white people. And when that happens, he said, "I tell you in the name of Jesus Christ, do not run, do not retaliate, do not resist; I tell you, *die!*"

The room erupted. There were protestations of every imaginable kind, some stupid, all irate, many well-reasoned, sensible. But clearly—in the new world etched out by Bill Stringfellow—each was wrong and irrelevant. We were now in his biblical world where the only realities were the presence of Christ in death and resurrection; no liberal strategies, no ecclesial pieties, rather the world of Christ dying in and to sin, with this mad American prophet asking if we were willing to do the same. Well, if this was what discipleship meant, we voted against it that night in that room. But at least we had seen it.

Prophets can be tolerated publicly if their discourse can be domesticated and routed into familiar paths of reform or redress. All his public life Bill Stringfellow was received into church circles as though he were a political liberal. He was understood to be, like them, a voice of reform, beseeching society to live up to its standards, a moralist dispensing helpful advice to this or that political problem. The reaction to Stringfellow that night was typical of other such occasions. The audience wanted the kind of useful advice which would help them solve political problems. Being asked to die clearly fell outside the realm of useful advice.

The confusion lay in misunderstanding Stringfellow's approach. In the seminary and throughout the church, the political purpose of biblical study was to learn how to take from scripture principles or morals which could then be applied to contemporary life. This was the classical Anglican and Roman Catholic approach. Stringfellow reversed the process. He studied the Bible and spoke from it with the purpose of *bringing us into* the biblical world. In that way we would understand our world, not as a separate enterprise, but enfolded in the ongoing biblical drama. In Bill Stringfellow, Augustine, and Calvin (refined through Karl Barth and Jacques Ellul) lived again.

It was not easy to position Bill Stringfellow politically in those days. Stringfellow's natural community, one to which he was tied by upbringing, education, and friendship, was among those thinking Christians who had learned their social and political views in the thirties and forties. They had been instructed by Reinhold Niebuhr and chastened by the experience of radical evil in Nazism, but their general approach was still intact. It was essentially moral. To the degree it was biblical, it drew from scripture moral principles which it then applied to the contemporary political scene. This, of course, meant that certain social goals were held to be compatible with—if not directly informed by—Christian values. Hence goodness, equality, popular participation, respect for others were believed to be at once biblical values and democratic values. A Christian enlisted in the struggle for the latter by borrowing from the former. This approach assumed a generally benign society (and in many ways, in spite of Reinhold Niebuhr, a benign view of human nature) simply in need of periodic reform. Reform came by instruction.

Stringfellow was no moralist and had little confidence in the power of mere instruction. Stringfellow did not teach, *he bore witness*. It was not his mission to solve political problems. He was called to testify to the freedom of Christians, in Christ, to live for those in the midst of debilitation and woe. His societal vision was darker, and, most importantly, he did not share the liberal assumption that society and individuals were basically in good order but from time to time needed proper instruction or advice to correct their faults.

In Stringfellow's biblical universe—which is, at the same time and in the deepest sense, our world—men and women are vectors in a titanic struggle not of good and evil but of death and resurrection. Social relations and political life embody this struggle in a greater and more congealed collective form. The world is held captive to the powers of death—sex, money, power, racism. Each power has the status of an idol, luring us into allegiance and dependence. None has any ultimate legitimacy or strength, but we do not know it because idols are so well camouflaged in a positive glow. They entice us and enslave us. We are all in the grip of some idol, some totalizing enticement. Salvation occurs not at the point of our choosing; indeed such is the power of death, we cannot choose against it. But we can be freed from it. Each principality or power is conquered, not with proper moral advice, but in the dying and rising of Christ. In Christ God took the "acolytes of death" to death itself. Only by faith in Christ can we be freed. Only in Christ can we rise from our essential thralldom to death. The main struggle therefore is not between good advice and bad advice but between death and resurrection. Grace is not knowledge or favor, some adjunctive divine aid to the already-formed person or society. Grace is the drama in which we are freed from the power of death itself in all those personal and social forms it takes, all personal and political occasions of occlusion.

For most of Stringfellow's life, he was welcomed by the church and was continually perceived in terms of the moralistic model. Episcopal bishops would invite him to speak to them about contemporary issues, thinking he would bolster some abstract liberal or moral position they had arrived at. He would speak and come to the conclusion, for example, that racism must end and be replaced by a society of radical equality, that the church should virtually give itself away in political struggle. The bishops would applaud. But there was always uneasiness in the room. This was because, while Stringfellow spoke of such a societal hope, his way of speaking about society, his biblical use and his dour apocalypticism did not correspond to any liberal notion and left the bishops uneasy. Where they sought a moral path to a better society, he beseeched a meta-historical vision of the Kingdom of God and the defeat of principalities, as accomplished at Calvary. It was not that the bishops were reactionary, though some were; it was that they were not biblical, had not re-focused their world in terms of the biblical struggle against principalities. As he joined them in the political struggle against racism and raged against the war in Vietnam—gaining some support—he was also chastising them for their easy accommodation to the structures of the world.

Though Stringfellow was at home in the world of radical critique, he was no radical. He was not unsympathetic to the leftward drift of many young radicals of his day, but he was chary of their increasingly ideological stance. Many on the Left had become radically democratic with the Port Huron Statement in 1962, but by the late sixties they began to drift to one or another form of anti-capitalist, socialist, or Marxist positions. These were natural shifts based on frustration.

The American political system could not or would not eradicate racism or end the war. It seemed only a radical critique along ideological lines could account for this recalcitrance. Hence the proliferation on the left of ideological groupings, each more radical than the other.

So long as ideology meant, as Karl Marx suggested, a set of fixed, seemingly benign societal ideas which served to cover (and justify) deeper forces of exploitation, Stringfellow was in agreement. His prophetic stance was by nature an exercise in unmasking. But in the hands of the young radicals, ideology turned into what Stringfellow feared the most, idolatry. Now ideas and perspectives became congealed and unassailable, new truths proposed, which were themselves rigid and abstract and, finally, covers for new power relationships. Ideology ceased to be an explanatory device, a general map to locate deeper evils; it became a set piece involving blind allegiance and repetitive enunciations. Stringfellow perceived among the young radicals the odor of death.

The younger radicals also made politics and the struggle for societal and political power the central human struggle, the main arena for human salvation. Stringfellow's uncompromising biblicism saw this as a monstrous inversion. He had learned from scripture of the ubiquitous and insistent power of principalities: those forces which impinge on men and women in the form of politics or personal relationships. He experienced these demonic forces in his own life. They could hardly be reduced to or confined to the political arena, any more than a liberal or radical politics could bring human redemption. Political forms could never be salvific. Racial integration or the restoration of legality (and peace) in foreign affairs were instances of the presence of Christ in this world. Politics could be in some sense transformed by witness and resistance. But political structures could never be rid of the corporate forms of sin. To break the power of the principalities, Stringfellow always adverted, not to a correct politics, but to the body of Christ and to the cross and empty grave of Jesus. The gospel (what he often called the Word of God) granted men and women a particular freedom to engage in politics and challenge what he called "the acolytes of death," but salvation preceded political reformation. Politics might be purged of its more insistent evil, but it could never be the locus of redemption. The primary struggle was not for the right politics but the defeat of the power of death in the Cross of Christ. Faith is freedom from these powers wherever they make their earthly appearance. It was at this point that radicals were suspicious of him. The only words they had were the most dismissive in the vocabulary of the day: "he's a liberal!"

The increasing politicization of the age led to another development which separated Stringfellow from political liberals and radicals within the church and society. If you grant to politics the central arena of meaning and redemption, then the scriptural categories of "principalities and powers" are reduced to the status of metaphors. One sees in scripture terms which merely point to or are symbolic substitutes for the primary reality of political power and political struggle. Stringfellow, however, believed the opposite. Political configurations as well as human quandaries were metaphors for the greater reality of the presence of principalities and powers. The presence of death in our world was the primary reality lived out among various personal and political acolytes.

At this point, few could follow Stringfellow. Few could take the scriptures this seriously. People liked the Bible for its beauty, its advice, its symbolic offerings, but to take the Bible at face value (which is not to say literally) was something few were willing to do. Stringfellow kept to his lonely path. He was admired, sought after, but few could fathom the man. To the end he remained idiosyncratic.

I remember when I last saw Bill Stringfellow. He came to give a talk in Milwaukee some time in 1973. We were aflame with rage at Nixon who was arrogantly misbehaving on a daily basis. The bombing of Vietnam was escalating and the usual lies were emanating from Washington. Stringfellow had by now written of the mendacity of Nixon's presidency and the supineness of the Congress and of what he thought was an illegal war. By now he was also identified with Daniel and Philip Berrigan, who had become folk heroes for the Catholic Left and others. We gathered expecting the usual diatribe against the war (though goodness knows what more could be said that had not already been said) and against Nixon. This time he sat at a table to speak. Once again, the talk was quiet, measured. Once again, he was not well. A church hall was packed. I remember noting especially the district attorney of Milwaukee, a devout Roman Catholic, a man wrestling with the war, his public duties, and his conscience. He truly wanted to hear Stringfellow's views. His eyes were riveted on Stringfellow as if hoping for a great deliverance.

Stringfellow began with a quote from the Book of Revelation. I recall a number of us grinning. We thought we were in for an apocalyptic thrashing of all our familiar political enemies. But no, it was not to be. Stringfellow, always the biblical man, was struck by a passage which spoke of the church being given more time before the end. We wanted a political rally; we got a Bible study. But you could see what was on his mind. He was not well, a certain energy was missing. His speech was ruminative not assaultive. He talked about the church and her protection by God, a protection clearly undeserved, yet nonetheless real. Why, he wondered? He unfolded for us the soiled, corrupt body of Christ, still, nonetheless, the locus of God's love and salvation. In the Book of Revelation it is the *state* (that is, politics of all kind) which is problematic. The *church* remains the antidote to politics which is inherently violent and unreformable. He touched here and there on contemporary politics but each time drew the remarks back to the church, that body where, in spite of all else, we find Christ and our peace. Of course, few in the audience had any notion what he was driving at. This was primarily a political audience, and—while they agreed the church was corrupt—they could not see how it was salvific. Long before dialectical thinking became theologically fashionable in America, Stringfellow was inhabiting this strange world of opposites. Americans, however, think discretely, chronologically, and exclusively. The audience still believed there was a "correct" politics which could be found and instituted. It was not a successful evening. The applause was generous, as much to honor his past politics, as they were remembered, and to express gratitude for his help for Dan Berrigan. But few really understood. He was brilliant, but here at the end he was as lonely and as unfathomable as when I had first met him. As the talk ended I looked over at the district attorney and saw him smile. I wondered if he had come away thinking as I did: the church is all we have.

CONTRIBUTORS

William R. Coats is Rector of St. Clement's Episcopal Church in Hawthorne, New Jersey. He is the author of *God in Public* and a frequent contributor to church publications.

Gary Commins is Rector of Holy Faith Episcopal Church in Inglewood, California, a multicultural congregation. He is the author of *Spiritual People/Radical Lives* (International Scholars Press, 1996), a comparative study of Dorothy Day, Martin Luther King, Jr., Thomas Merton, and A. J. Muste.

John M. Gessell is Professor Emeritus of Christian Ethics, the University of the South, Sewanee, Tennessee. He served as Editor of the *St. Luke's Journal of Theology* from 1976 to 1990.

James E. Griffiss, a priest in the Episcopal Church, is Editor of the *Anglican Theological Review* and Visiting Professor of Theology at Seabury-Western Theological Seminary in Evanston, Illinois. He is the author and editor of several books, most recently, *Naming the Mystery*. He is editor of a selection of writings from Archbishop of Canterbury Michael Ramsey, *To Believe is to Pray*, published in 1997 by Cowley Publications.

Jeffrey A. Mackey was ordained a priest in the Episcopal Church in 1993, after nineteen years as a pastor in the Christian & Missionary Alliance. He is currently the Rector of Trinity Episcopal Church, DeRidder, Louisiana, and Vicar of Polk Memorial Church, Leesville, Louisiana. He is also Professor of Pastoral Ministry at the Cranmer Theological House in Shreveport, Louisiana. He holds the Doctor of Ministry degree from the Graduate Theological Foundation where he is also a Ph.D. Candidate Fellow. His dissertation will center on the place of William Stringfellow in the scheme of Anglican moral theology.

Andrew W. McThenia, Jr., is James P. Morefield Professor of Law at Washington and Lee University, Lexington, Virginia, teaching on contracts, the lawyer's role, legislation, and mental disabilities. He works with religious communities and congregations and others who find themselves resisting the initiatives of the mainstream culture. McThenia is the author of several books, including *Radical Christian and Exemplary Lawyer: Honoring William Stringfellow* (Eerdmans, 1995) and serves as chair of the Episcopal Church Publishing Company, publisher of *The Witness*.

Jacqueline Schmitt is Episcopal Chaplain at Northwestern University, Evanston, Illinois, and the Editor of *Plumbline*, a journal of ministry in higher education.

Timothy F. Sedgwick is Professor of Christian Ethics at Virginia Theological Seminary. Formerly, he was Professor of Christian Ethics and Moral Theology at Seabury-Western Theological Seminary in Evanston, Illinois. He is the author of *The Making of Ministry* (Cowley, 1993), *The Crisis in Moral Teaching in the Episcopal Church* (with Philip Turner; Morehouse, 1992), and *Sacramental Ethics: Paschal Identity and the Christian Life*.

Gardiner H. Shattuck, Jr., chairs the governing board and teaches Church History at the School for Ministries of the Diocese of Rhode Island. He is currently writing a book on the history of the Episcopal Church and American racism, tentatively titled *Dwelling Together in Unity: Episcopalians and the Dilemmas of Race, 1943-1973*.

Robert Boak Slocum is Rector of Church of the Holy Communion in Lake Geneva, Wisconsin, and a Lecturer in Theology at Marquette University, Milwaukee, Wisconsin. He recently completed a doctorate in Systematic Theology at Marquette. He was co-editor of *Documents of Witness: A History of the Episcopal Church, 1782-1985* (Church Hymnal, 1994). He also serves as co-editor of a concise encyclopedia of the Episcopal Church and recently completed a book on the theology of William Porcher DuBose.

Bill Wylie-Kellermann is a United Methodist pastor teaching at the Whitaker School of Theology in Detroit. He is author of *Seasons of Faith and Conscience* (Orbis, 1991) and Editor of *A Keeper of the Word: Selected Writings of William Stringfellow* (Eerdmans, 1994) in which most of the above quotations may be found. He is at work on a book concerning the principalities and, with Andrew McThenia, on a Stringfellow biography.

A STRINGFELLOW BIBLIOGRAPHY

BOOKS BY WILLIAM STRINGFELLOW

Count It All Joy. Grand Rapids, Michigan: William B. Eerdmans Publishing, 1967.

(With Anthony Towne.) *The Bishop Pike Affair: Scandals of Conscience, Heresy, Relevance and Solemnity in the Contemporary Church*. New York: Harper and Row, 1967.

Conscience and Obedience. Waco, Texas: Word Books, Inc., 1977.

Count It All Joy. Grand Rapids, Michigan: William B. Eerdmans Publishing Company, 1967.

(With Anthony Towne.) *The Death and Life of Bishop Pike*. Garden City, New York: Doubleday, 1976.

Dissenter in a Great Society. New York: Holt, Rinehart and Winston, 1966.

An Ethic for Christians and Other Aliens in a Strange Land. Waco, Texas: Word Books, Inc., 1973.

Free in Obedience. New York: Seabury Press, 1964.

Impostors of God: Inquiries into Favorite Idols. Washington, D.C.: Witness Books, 1969.

Instead of Death. New York: Seabury Press, 1963. Second ed., New York: Seabury Press, 1976.

My People Is the Enemy. New York: Holt, Rinehart and Winston, Inc., 1964.

The Politics of Spirituality. Louisville, Kentucky: Westminster Press, 1984.

A Private and Public Faith. Grand Rapids, Michigan: William B. Eerdmans Publishing Company, 1962.

A Second Birthday. Garden City, New York: Doubleday, 1970.

A Simplicity of Faith: My Experience in Mourning. Nashville: Abingdon Press, 1982.

(With Anthony Towne.) *Suspect Tenderness: The Ethics of the Berrigan Witness.* New York: Holt, Rinehart and Winston, 1971.

BOOKS CONCERNING WILLIAM STRINGFELLOW

Andrew W. McThenia, Jr., ed. *Radical Christian and Exemplary Lawyer: A Festschrift Honoring William Stringfellow.* Grand Rapids, Michigan: William B. Eerdmans Publishing, 1995.

Bill Wylie-Kellermann, ed. *A Keeper of the Word: Selected Writings of William Stringfellow.* Grand Rapids, Michigan: William B. Eerdmans Publishing, 1994.